Machiavelli Was Wrong:
It is Better to Be Loved

By Eric Michael Moberg

2016

Prescott University Press

ISBN: 978-1540437204

Notes from the 2016 Campaign Trail

Excerpts from and explication of

The Prince

Niccolo Machiavelli
translated by N.H. Thomson
The Harvard Classics
edited by Charles W. Eliot
New York: P.F. Collier & Son, 1909–14

Machiavelli's Dedication

To the Magnificent Lorenzo di Piero de' Medici

Introduction

History proves Machiavelli wrong about his most famous claim that it is better to be feared than loved as a leader.[1] This question could hardly be more relevant in the age of simultaneous wars on "drugs" and "terror," not to mention the presidential campaigns of 2016, featuring such contrasting characters as the "catastrophe of neo-fascism" in Donald Trump, the "disaster of neo-liberalism" in Hillary Clinton,[2] the "democratic socialism" of Bernie Sanders, the "progressivism" of Jill Stein, and the "pragmatic libertarianism" of Gary Johnson.

As Machiavelli explains in chapter XXII below:

A Prince should therefore disregard the reproach of being thought cruel where it enables him to keep his subjects united and obedient. For he who quells disorder by a very few signal examples will in the end be more merciful than he who from too great leniency permits things to take their course and so to result in rapine and bloodshed; for these hurt the whole State, whereas the severities of the Prince injure individuals only.

But, the Declaration of Independence, the Federalist Papers, and the United States Constitution all reject the refusal to respect individual and minority rights espoused later by Napoleon, Stalin, Nixon, Putin, and Cheney in a Machiavellian world where each and every state, regardless of pretenses to socialism or democracy, is a dictatorship.[3] Dictatorship banks on fear while crushing love. This is nothing new, only the names change. We can and must fight this

---

[1] For an interesting discussion of the current practical application of Machiavelli's theory, see: Kinkopf, Neil. "Is it Better to Be Loved or Feared? Some Thought on Lessons Learned from the Presidency of George W. Bush." *Duke Journal of Constitutional Law & Public Policy* 4, (January 2009): 45-55

[2] Cornel West, *Democracy Now*, 18 January 2016

[3] Bates, Thomas R. "Gramsci and the Theory of Hegemony." *Journal of the History of Ideas* 36, no. 2 (1975): 351-66.

spiral into extinction. Another world is possible—a world built on love.

Eric Michael Moberg
San Francisco 2016

Machiavelli begins his famous 33,000-word essay, *The Prince*, with fawning language that fetishizes hierarchy and cult of personality in a pathetically obsequious pandering to Lorenzo di Piero de' Medici in order to re-ingratiate himself to the ruling family of the day.

IT is customary for such as seek a Prince's favor, to present themselves before him with those things of theirs which they themselves most value, or in which they perceive him chiefly to delight. Accordingly, we often see horses, armor, cloth of gold, precious stones, and the like costly gifts, offered to Princes as worthy of their greatness. Desiring in like manner to approach your Magnificence with some token of my devotion, I have found among my possessions none that I so much prize and esteem as a knowledge of the actions of great men, acquired in the course of a long experience of modern affairs and a continual study of antiquity. Which knowledge most carefully and patiently pondered over and sifted by me, and now reduced into this little book, I send to your Magnificence. And though I deem the work unworthy of your greatness, yet am I bold enough to hope that your courtesy will dispose you to accept it, considering that I can offer you no better gift than the means of mastering in a very brief time, all that in the course of so many years, and at the cost of so many hardships and dangers, I have learned, and know.

Machiavelli then proceeds to feign humility.

This work I have not adorned or amplified with rounded periods, swelling and high-flown language, or any other of those extrinsic attractions and allurements wherewith many authors are wont to set off and grace their writings; since it is my desire that it should either pass wholly un-honored, or that the truth of its matter and the importance of its subject should alone recommend it.

And, it is not until the third paragraph of his introduction that Machiavelli even mentions "the People" to whom the Prince "should belong...."

Nor would I have it thought presumption that a person of very mean and humble station should venture to discourse and lay down rules concerning the government of Princes. For as those who make maps of countries place themselves low down in the plains to study the character of mountains and elevated lands, and place themselves high up on the mountains to get a better view of the plains, so in like manner to understand the People a man should be a Prince, and to have a clear notion of Princes he should belong to the People.

Machiavelli quickly returns to groveling, though, in the fourth paragraph, with dripping honorifics and tribute to the Medici family.

Let your Magnificence, then, accept this little gift in the spirit in which I offer it; wherein, if you diligently read and study it, you will recognize my extreme desire that you should attain to that eminence which Fortune and your own merits promise you. Should you from the height of your greatness some time turn your eyes to these humble regions, you will become aware how undeservedly I have to endure the keen and unremitting malignity of Fortune.

I.   Of the Various Kinds of Princedom, and of the Ways in Which They Are Acquired

ALL the States and Governments by which men are or ever have been ruled, have been and are either Republics or Princedoms. Princedoms are either hereditary, in which the sovereignty is derived through an ancient line of ancestors, or they are new. New Princedoms are either wholly new, as that of Milan to Francesco Sforza; or they are like limbs joined on to the hereditary possessions of the Prince who acquires them, as the Kingdom of Naples to the dominions of the King of Spain. The States thus acquired have either been used to live under a Prince or have been free; and he who acquires them does so either by his own arms or by the arms of others, and either by good fortune or by merit.

Clinton seeks her 2016 Princedom in a version of heredity through the "ancestry" of her husband.[4] Trump seeks his by threat to employ "the arms of others," namely the United States military.[5] Sanders, on the other hand, mostly rejects both nepotism and militarism[6] in his quest, as do Johnson[7] and Stein.[8] Machiavelli's dichotomy of heredity or conquest, therefore, improperly limits humanity to choices that perpetuate elitism and state violence.

In fact, it was not ever thus. Prior to Machiavelli, many societies organized around principles other than heredity or conquest. As Buddha revealed, "Better than a thousand hollow words, is one word that brings peace."

---

[4] Wolfgang, Ben. "Clinton Tries to Steady Campaign, Touts Husband's Economic Record in N.H." *Washington Times,* 2 February 2016.

[5] "Lieu: 'Trump said I know more about Isis than the Generals do.'" *CNBC*, 28 July 2016.

[6] Maddow, Rachel. "Sen. Sanders Urges Caution, Planning on ISIS." *MSNBC*, 10 September 2014.

[7] "A Transcript of The Washington Post Editorial Board's Meeting with Gary Johnson and William Weld." *Washington Post*, 7 July 2016.

[8] "Jill Stein on War & Peace." *On The Issues*. 30 July 2016.

American gang leaders, or war lords, set brave examples of peace through truces in Los Angeles in 1992 and 2016 in Baltimore[9] in response to ruthless state violence perpetrated by sworn police officers.[10]

[9] Woods, Baynard. "Baltimore's Uprising: Rival Gangs Push for Peace After Freddie Gray's Death." *The Guardian*, 27 April 2016.
[10] Rodríguez, Dylan. "De-provincialising Police Violence: on the Recent Events at UC Davis." *Race & Class* 54, no. 1 (July 2012): 99-109.

II.   Of Hereditary Princedoms of Republics

Here I shall treat exclusively of Princedoms, and, filling in the outline above traced out, shall proceed to examine how such States are to be governed and maintained.

I say, then, that hereditary States, accustomed to the family of their Prince, are maintained with far less difficulty than new States, since all that is required is that the Prince shall not depart from the usages of his ancestors, trusting for the rest to deal with events as they arise. So that if an hereditary Prince be of average address, he will always maintain himself in his Princedom, unless deprived of it by some extraordinary and irresistible force; and even if so deprived will recover it, should any, even the least, mishap overtake the usurper. We have in Italy an example of this in the Duke of Ferrara, who never could have withstood the attacks of the Venetians in 1484, nor those of Pope Julius in 1510, had not his authority in that State been consolidated by time. For since a Prince by birth has fewer occasions and less need to give offence, he ought to be better loved, and will naturally be popular with his subjects unless outrageous vices make him odious. Moreover, the very antiquity and continuance of his rule will efface the memories and causes which lead to innovation. For one change always leaves a dovetail into which another will fit.

Machiavelli continues his monarchic assumptions and deference of heredity and militarism. Clinton and Trump, too, trade on family names, dynastic assumption, and overtaking "usurpers," such as Bernie Sanders.[11]

Even in the fifteenth century, though, alternatives existed to primogeniture, monarchy, and militarism. The Greeks, Romans, and

---

[11] Lynch, Conor. "Bernie Sanders is no Spoiler: He's Trying to Cure the Centrist Complacency That's Plaguing the Democratic Party." *Salon*, 21 June 2016.

Germanic tribes[12] had experimented with various forms of democracy and republicanism, not to mention fourteenth and fifteenth century republics in Florence and Venice. As for peace or neutrality, Saint Francis of Assisi echoed the teachings of Jesus well by urging, "Lord, make me an instrument of thy peace. Where there is hatred, let me sow love."

---

[12] Gillin, J. L. "The Origin of Democracy." *American Journal of Sociology* 24, no. 6 (1919): 704-14.

III. Of Mixed Princedoms

BUT in new Princedoms difficulties abound. And, first, if the Princedom be not wholly new, but joined on to the ancient dominions of the Prince, so as to form with them what may be termed a mixed Princedom, changes will come from a cause common to all new States, namely, that men, thinking to better their condition, are always ready to change masters, and in this expectation will take up arms against any ruler; wherein they deceive themselves, and find afterwards by experience that they are worse off than before. This again results naturally and necessarily from the circumstance that the Prince cannot avoid giving offence to his new subjects, either in respect of the troops he quarters on them, or of some other of the numberless vexations attendant on a new acquisition. And in this way you may find that you have enemies in all those whom you have injured in seizing the Princedom, yet cannot keep the friendship of those who helped you to gain it; since you can neither reward them as they expect, nor yet, being under obligations to them, use violent remedies against them. For however strong you may be in respect of your army, it is essential that in entering a new Province you should have the good will of its inhabitants.

Hence it happened that Louis XII of France, speedily gaining possession of Milan, as speedily lost it; and that on the occasion of its first capture, Lodovico Sforza was able with his own forces only to take it from him. For the very people who had opened the gates to the French King, when they found themselves deceived in their expectations and hopes of future benefits, could not put up with the insolence of their new ruler. True it is that when a State rebels and is again got under, it will not afterwards be lost so easily. For the Prince, using the rebellion as a pretext, will not scruple to secure himself by punishing the guilty, bringing the suspected to trial, and otherwise strengthening his position in the points where it was weak. So that if to recover Milan from the French it was enough on the first occasion that a Duke Lodovico should raise alarms on the frontiers to wrest it from them a second time the whole world had to be ranged against them, and their armies destroyed and driven out of Italy. And this for the reasons above assigned. And yet, for a second time, Milan was lost to the King. The general causes of its first loss have been shown. It remains to note the causes of the second, and to point out the remedies which the French King had, or which might have been used by another in like circumstances to maintain his conquest more successfully than he did. I say, then, that those States which upon their acquisition are joined on to the ancient dominions of the Prince who acquires them, are either of the same Province and tongue as the people of these dominions, or they are not. When they are, there is a great ease in retaining them, especially when they have not been accustomed to live in freedom. To hold them securely it is enough to have rooted out the line of the reigning Prince; because if in other respects the old condition of things be continued, and there be no discordance in their customs, men live peaceably with one another, as we see to have been the case in Brittany, Burgundy, Gascony, and Normandy, which have so long been united to France. For although there be some slight difference in their languages, their customs are similar, and they can easily get on together. He, therefore, who acquires such a State, if he means to keep it, must see to two things; first, that the blood of the ancient line of Princes be destroyed; second, that no change be made in respect of laws or taxes; for in this way the newly acquired State speedily becomes incorporated with the hereditary.

But when States are acquired in a country differing in language, usages, and laws, difficulties multiply, and great good fortune, as well as address, is needed to overcome them. One of the best and most efficacious methods for dealing with such a State, is for the Prince who acquires it to go and dwell there in person, since this will tend to make his tenure more secure and lasting. This course has been followed by the Turk with regard to Greece, who, had he not, in addition to all his other precautions for securing that Province, himself come to live in it, could never have kept his hold of it. For when you are on the spot, disorders are detected in their beginnings and remedies can be readily applied; but when you are at a distance, they are not heard of until they have gathered strength and the case is past cure. Moreover, the Province in which you take up your abode is not pillaged by your officers; the people are pleased to have a ready recourse to their Prince; and have all the more reason if they are well disposed, to love, if disaffected, to fear him. A foreign enemy desiring to attack that State would be cautious how he did so. In short, where the Prince resides in person, it will be extremely difficult to oust him.

Another excellent expedient is to send colonies into one or two places, so that these may become, as it were, the keys of the Province; for you must either do this, or else keep up a numerous force of men-at-arms and foot soldiers. A Prince need not spend much on colonies. He can send them out and support them at little or no charge to himself, and the only persons to whom he gives offence are those whom he deprives of their fields and houses to bestow them on the new inhabitants. Those who are thus injured form but a small part of the community, and remaining scattered and poor can never become dangerous. All others being left unmolested, are in consequence easily quieted, and at the same time are afraid to make a false move, lest they share the fate of those who have been deprived of their possessions. In few words, these colonies cost less than soldiers, are more faithful, and give less offence, while those who are offended, being, as I have said, poor and dispersed, cannot hurt. And let it here be noted that men are either to be kindly treated, or utterly crushed, since they can revenge lighter injuries, but not graver. Wherefore the injury we do to a man should be of a sort to leave no fear of reprisals. But if instead of colonies you send troops, the cost is vastly greater, and the whole revenues of the country are spent in guarding it; so that the gain becomes a loss, and much deeper offence is given; since in shifting the quarters of your soldiers from place to place the whole country suffers hardship, which as all feel, all are made enemies; and enemies who remaining, although vanquished, in their own homes, have power to hurt. In every way, therefore, this mode of defense is as disadvantageous as that by colonizing is useful.

The Prince who establishes himself in a Province whose laws and language differ from those of his own people, ought also to make himself the head and protector of his feebler neighbors, and endeavor to weaken the stronger, and must see that by no accident shall any other stranger as powerful as himself find an entrance there. For it will always happen that some such person will be called in by those of the Province who are discontented either through ambition or fear; as we see of old the Romans brought into Greece by the Aetolians, and in every other country that they entered, invited there by its inhabitants. And the usual course of things is that so soon as a formidable stranger enters a Province, all the weaker powers side with him, moved thereto by the ill-will they bear towards him who has hitherto kept them in subjection. So that in respect of these lesser powers, no trouble is needed to gain them over, for at once, together, and of their own accord, they throw in their lot with the government of the stranger. The new Prince, therefore, has only to see that they do not increase too much in strength, and with his own forces, aided by their good will, can easily subdue any who are powerful, so as to remain supreme in the Province. He who does not manage this matter well, will soon lose whatever he has gained, and while he retains it will find in it endless troubles and annoyances.

In dealing with the countries of which they took possession the Romans diligently followed the methods I have described. They planted colonies, conciliated weaker powers without adding to their strength, humbled the great, and never suffered a formidable stranger to acquire influence. A single example will suffice to show this. In Greece the Romans took the Achaians and Aetolians into their pay; the Macedonian monarchy was humbled; Antiochus was driven out. But the services of the Achaians and Aetolians never obtained for them any addition to their power; no persuasions on the part of Philip could induce the Romans to be his friends on the condition of sparing him humiliation; nor could all the power of Antiochus bring them to consent to his exercising any authority within that Province. And in thus acting the Romans did as all wise rulers should, who have to consider not only present difficulties but also future, against which they must use all diligence to provide; for these, if they be foreseen while yet remote, admit of easy remedy, but if their approach be awaited, are already past cure, the disorder having become hopeless; realizing what the physicians tell us of hectic fever, that in its beginning it is easy to cure, but hard to recognize; whereas, after a time, not having been detected and treated at the first, it becomes easy to recognize but impossible to cure. And so it is with State affairs. For the distempers of a State being discovered while yet inchoate, which can only be done by a sagacious ruler, may easily be dealt with; but when, from not being observed, they are suffered to grow until they are obvious to everyone, there is no longer any remedy. The Romans, therefore, foreseeing evils while they were yet far off, always provided against them, and never suffered them to take their course for the sake of avoiding war; since they knew that war is not so to be avoided, but is only postponed to the advantage of the other side. They chose, therefore, to make war with Philip and Antiochus in Greece, that they might not have to make it with them in Italy, although for a while they might have escaped both. This they did not desire, nor did the maxim leave it to Time, which the wise men of our own day have always on their lips, ever recommend itself to them. What they looked to enjoy were the fruits of their own valor and foresight. For Time, driving all things before it, may bring with it evil as well as good.

But let us now go back to France and examine whether she has followed any of those methods of which I have made mention. I shall speak of Louis and not of Charles, because from the former having held longer possession of Italy, his manner of acting is more plainly seen. You will find, then, that he has done the direct opposite of what he should have done in order to retain a foreign State.

King Louis was brought into Italy by the ambition of the Venetians, who hoped by his coming to gain for themselves a half of the State of Lombardy. I will not blame this coming, nor the part taken by the King, because, desiring to gain a footing in Italy, where he had no friends, but on the contrary, owing to the conduct of Charles, every door was shut against him, he was driven to accept such friendships as he could get. And his designs might easily have succeeded had he not made mistakes in other particulars of conduct.

By the recovery of Lombardy, Louis at once regained the credit which Charles had lost. Genoa made submission; the Florentines came to terms; the Marquis of Mantua, the Duke of Ferrara, the Bentivogli, the Countess of Forli, the Lords of Faenza, Pesaro, Rimini, Camerino, and Piombino, the citizens of Lucca, Pisa, and Siena, all came forward offering their friendship. The Venetians, who to obtain possession of a couple of towns in Lombardy had made the French King master of two-thirds of Italy, had now cause to repent the rash game they had played.

Let anyone, therefore, consider how easily King Louis might have maintained his authority in Italy had he observed the rules which I have noted above, and secured and protected all those friends of his, who being weak, and fearful, some of the Church, some of the Venetians, were of necessity obliged to attach themselves to him, and with whose assistance, for they were many, he might readily have made himself safe against any other powerful State. But no sooner was he in Milan than he took a contrary course, in helping Pope Alexander to occupy Romagna; not perceiving that in seconding this enterprise he weakened himself by alienating friends and those who had thrown themselves into his arms, while he strengthened the Church by adding great temporal power to the spiritual power which of itself confers so mighty an authority. Making this first mistake, he was forced to follow it up, until at last, in order to curb the ambition of Pope Alexander, and prevent him becoming master of Tuscany, he was obliged to come himself into Italy.

And as though it were not enough for him to have aggrandized the Church and stripped himself of friends, he must needs in his desire to possess the Kingdom of Naples, divide it with the King of Spain; thus bringing into Italy, where before he had been supreme, a rival to whom the ambitious and discontented in that Province might have recourse. And whereas he might have left in Naples a King willing to hold as his tributary, he displaced him to make way for another strong enough to effect his expulsion. The wish to acquire is no doubt a natural and common sentiment, and when men attempt things within their power, they will always be praised rather than blamed. But when they persist in attempts that are beyond their power, mishaps and blame ensue. If France, therefore, with her own forces could have attacked Naples, she should have done so. If she could not, she ought not to have divided it. And if her partition of Lombardy with the Venetians may be excused as the means whereby a footing was gained in Italy, this other partition is to be condemned as not justified by the like necessity.

Louis, then, had made these five blunders. He had destroyed weaker States, he had strengthened a Prince already strong, he had brought into the country a very powerful stranger, he had not come to reside, and he had not sent colonies. And yet all these blunders might not have proved disastrous to him while he lived, had he not added to them a sixth in depriving the Venetians of their dominions. For had he neither aggrandized the Church, nor brought Spain into Italy, it might have been at once reasonable and necessary to humble the Venetians; but after committing himself to these other courses, he should never have consented to the ruin of Venice. For while the Venetians were powerful, they would always have kept others back from an attempt on Lombardy, as well because they never would have agreed to that enterprise on any terms save of themselves being made its masters, as because others would never have desired to take it from France in order to hand it over to them, nor would ever have ventured to defy both. And if it be said that King Louis ceded Romagna to Alexander, and Naples to Spain in order to avoid war, I answer that for the reasons already given, you ought never to suffer your designs to be crossed in order to avoid war, since war is not so to be avoided, but is only deferred to your disadvantage. And if others should allege the King's promise to the Pope to undertake that enterprise on his behalf, in return for the dissolution of his marriage, and for the Cardinal's hat conferred on d'Amboise, I answer by referring to what I say further on concerning the faith of Princes and how it is to be kept.

King Louis, therefore, lost Lombardy from not following any one of the methods pursued by others who have taken Provinces with the resolve to keep them. Nor is this anything strange, but only what might reasonably and naturally be looked for. And on this very subject I spoke to d'Amboise at Nantes, at the time when Duke Valentino, as Cesare Borgia, son to Pope Alexander, was vulgarly called, was occupying Romagna. For, on the Cardinal saying to me that the Italians did not understand war, I answered that the French did not understand statecraft, for had they done so, they never would have allowed the Church to grow so powerful. And the event shows that the aggrandizement of the Church and of Spain in Italy has been brought about by France, and that the ruin of France has been wrought by them. Whence we may draw the general axiom, which never or rarely errs, that he who is the cause of another's greatness is to cause himself to be undone, since he must work either by address or force, each of which excites distrust in the person raised to power.

Sadly absent from Machiavelli's advice on what amount to colonial wars of aggression is any analysis as to the basic morality of invading surrounding territories. Instead, Machiavelli coldly assumes that "war is not…to be avoided" and advises that invaders "see…that the blood of the ancient line of Princes be destroyed" so as to prevent the conquered government from regaining power once the people form a dislike for the new ruthless rulers. The "Prince" can accomplish annexation in the cheap, according to Machiavelli simply by having his armies steal the land of the former citizens and occupy "their fields and houses to bestow them on the new inhabitants." In summation, Machiavelli sees statecraft as a zero sum game in which to "cause of another's greatness is" to cause "himself to be undone."

While Trump and Clinton clearly ascribe to this necessity for war, Stein, Johnson, and Sanders wisely speak of diplomacy first. Given the complexity of warfare in the nuclear age and such potential adversaries as Russia, China, and Iran, the dangers of such belligerence could lead to thermonuclear annihilation[13] of the human species and even the planet.

Many leaders and philosophers before and after Machiavelli warned of the immorality of war and wisdom of peace.[14] Even modern popular poets such as Jimi Hendrix offer saner visions: "When the power of love overcomes the love of power the world will know peace."

---

[13] Broad, Willian and David E. Sanger. "Race for Latest Class of Nuclear Arms Threatens to Revive Cold War." *New York Times*, 16 April 2016.
[14] Trueblood, Benjamin F. "The Historic Development of the Peace Idea." *The Advocate of Peace (1894-1920)* 67, no. 10 (1905): 224-30.

IV. Why the Kingdom of Darius, Conquered by Alexander, Did Not, on Alexander's Death, Rebel Against His Successors

ALEXANDER THE GREAT having achieved the conquest of Asia in a few years, and dying before he had well entered on possession, it might have been expected, having regard to the difficulty of preserving newly acquired States, that on his death the whole country would rise in revolt. Nevertheless, his successors were able to keep their hold, and found in doing so no other difficulty than arose from their own ambition and mutual jealousies.

If anyone think this strange and ask the cause, I answer, that all the Princedoms of which we have record have been governed in one or other of two ways, either by a sole Prince, all others being his servants permitted by his grace and favor to assist in governing the kingdom as his ministers; or else, by a Prince with his Barons who hold their rank, not by the favor of a superior Lord, but by antiquity of blood, and who have States and subjects of their own who recognize them as their rulers and entertain for them a natural affection. States governed by a sole Prince and by his servants vest in him a more complete authority; because throughout the land none but he is recognized as sovereign, and if obedience be yielded to any others, it is yielded as to his ministers and officers for whom personally no special love is felt.

Of these two forms of government we have examples in our own days in the Turk and the King of France. The whole Turkish empire is governed by a sole Prince, all others being his slaves. Dividing his kingdom into sandjaks, he sends thither different governors whom he shifts and changes at his pleasure. The King of France, on the other hand, is surrounded by a multitude of nobles of ancient descent, each acknowledged and loved by subjects of his own, and each asserting a precedence in rank of which the King can deprive him only at his peril.

He, therefore, who considers the different character of these two States, will perceive that it would be difficult to gain possession of that of the Turk, but that once won it might be easily held. The obstacles to its conquest are that the invader cannot be called in by a native nobility, nor expect his enterprise to be aided by the defection of those whom the sovereign has around him. And this for the various reasons already given, namely, that all being slaves and under obligations they are not easily corrupted, or if corrupted can render little assistance, being unable, as I have already explained, to carry the people with them. Whoever, therefore, attacks the Turk must reckon on finding a united people, and must trust rather to his own strength than to divisions on the other side. But were his adversary once overcome and defeated in the field, so that he could not repair his armies, no cause for anxiety would remain, except in the family of the Prince; which being extirpated, there would be none else to fear; for since all beside are without credit with the people, the invader, as before his victory he had nothing to hope from them, so after it has nothing to dread.

But the contrary is the case in kingdoms governed like that of France, into which, because men who are discontented and desirous of change are always to be found, you may readily procure an entrance by gaining over some Baron of the Realm. Such persons, for the reasons already given, are able to open the way to you for the invasion of their country and to render its conquest easy. But afterwards the effort to hold your ground involves you in endless difficulties, as well in respect of those who have helped you, as of those whom you have overthrown. Nor will it be enough to have destroyed the family of the Prince, since all those other Lords remain to put themselves at the head of new movements; whom being unable either to content or to destroy, you lose the State whenever occasion serves them. Now, if you examine the nature of the government of Darius, you will find that it resembled that of the Turk, and, consequently, that it was necessary for Alexander, first of all, to defeat him utterly and strip him of his dominions; after which defeat, Darius having died, the country, for the causes above explained, was permanently secured to Alexander. And had his successors continued united they might have enjoyed it undisturbed, since there arose no disorders in that kingdom save those of their own creating.

But kingdoms ordered like that of France cannot be retained with the same ease. Hence the repeated risings of Spain, Gaul, and Greece against the Romans, resulting from the number of small Princedoms of which these Provinces were made up. For while the memory of these lasted, the Romans could never think their tenure safe. But when that memory was worn out by the authority and long continuance of their rule, they gained a secure hold, and were able afterwards in their contests among themselves, each to carry with him some portion of these Provinces, according as each had acquired influence there; for these, on the extinction of the line of their old Princes, came to recognize no other Lords than the Romans.

Bearing all this in mind, no one need wonder at the ease wherewith Alexander was able to lay a firm hold on Asia, nor that Pyrrhus and many others found difficulty in preserving other acquisitions; since this arose, not from the less or greater merit of the conquerors, but from the different character of the States with which they had to deal.

Machiavelli clarifies his recommendation for ruling a state not simply by autocracy or monarchy but by a single monarch not even willing to share some power with barons or other lesser aristocrats, lest the "subjects" might confuse or dilute their obedience. Trump, too, touts the cult of personality[15] in the case of Alexander the Great, not once considering the possibility of democracy or freedom. Late July 2016 revelations of party subterfuge by Clinton surrogates in the media[16] and the Democratic National Committee to undermine Sanders campaign, similarly, demonstrate Clinton's disdain for

---

[15] Cadei, Emily. "Cult of Personality: How Trump Uses the Playbook of Europe's Far Right." *Newsweek*, 10 May 2016.

[16] Bump, Philip. "Why the Associated Press Called the Race for Hillary Clinton When Nobody Was Looking." *Washington Post*, June 2016.

democracy. More instructive still was Clinton's response to the scandal—instead of condemning Wasserman-Schultz for corruption, Clinton praised the scoundrel and immediately hired her into a key position in the Clinton campaign.[17] Around the same time, Libertarian candidate Johnson and Green Party candidate Stein surged in national polls[18] to record highs for their parties. Erdogan's July 2016 purges[19] represent an eerie echo to Machiavelli's reference to the Turks as slaves under one ruler. Perhaps most revolting is Machiavelli's reverence for the Romans and their empire.

---

[17] Zeleny, Jeff, MJ Lee, and Eric Bradner. "Dems Open Convention without Wasserman Schultz. *CNN*, 25 July 2016.

[18] Walsh, Kenneth T. "Libertarian Nominee Gary Johnson Says Both Political Parties Failing Voters." *U.S. News and World Reports*, 29 July 2016.

[19] Srivastava, Mehul. "Recep Tayyip Erdogan's Purge Extends from Soldiers to a Stock Analyst." *Financial Times*, 28 July 2016.

V. How Cities or Provinces Which before Their Acquisition Have Lived under Their Own Laws Are to Be Governed

WHEN a newly acquired State has been accustomed, as I have said, to live under its own laws and in freedom, there are three methods whereby it may be held. The first is to destroy it; the second, to go and reside there in person; the third, to suffer it to live on under its own laws, subjecting it to a tribute, and entrusting its government to a few of the inhabitants who will keep the rest your friends. Such a Government, since it is the creature of the new Prince, will see that it cannot stand without his protection and support, and must therefore do all it can to maintain him; and a city accustomed to live in freedom, if it is to be preserved at all, is more easily controlled through its own citizens than in any other way.

We have examples of all these methods in the histories of the Spartans and the Romans. The Spartans held Athens and Thebes by creating oligarchies in these cities, yet lost them in the end. The Romans, to retain Capua, Carthage, and Numantia, destroyed them and never lost them. On the other hand, when they thought to hold Greece as the Spartans had held it, leaving it its freedom and allowing it to be governed by its own laws, they failed, and had to destroy many cities of that Province before they could secure it. For, in truth, there is no sure way of holding other than by destroying, and whoever becomes master of a City accustomed to live in freedom and does not destroy it, may reckon on being destroyed by it. For if it should rebel, it can always screen itself under the name of liberty and its ancient laws, which no length of time, nor any benefits conferred will ever cause it to forget; and do what you will, and take what care you may, unless the inhabitants be scattered and dispersed, this name, and the old order of things, will never cease to be remembered, but will at once be turned against you whenever misfortune overtakes you, as when Pisa rose against the Florentines after a hundred years of servitude. If, however, the newly acquired City or Province has been accustomed to live under a Prince, and his line is extinguished, it will be impossible for the citizens, used, on the one hand, to obey, and deprived, on the other, of their old ruler, to agree to choose a leader from among themselves; and as they know not how to live as freemen, and are therefore slow to take up arms, a stranger may readily gain them over and attach them to his cause. But in Republics there is a stronger vitality, a fiercer hatred, a keener thirst for revenge. The memory of their former freedom will not let them rest; so that the safest course is either to destroy them, or to go and live in them.

Machiavelli entirely ignores leaving free people free and simply negotiating and trading with them. Clinton's track record as Secretary of State, supporting rebellion in Libya—where many owned guns[20] and most enjoyed a high standard of living—and the coup in Honduras[21] would make Machiavelli as proud as Trump's boastful saber rattling[22] at countries that he likely could not find on a globe. Johnson, on the other hand, calls for a much more conservative and isolationist approach, while Stein[23] envisions a cooperative and respectful foreign policy that dismantles its military empire and relies on diplomacy instead. Sanders' foreign policy is more complex but less hawkish than Clinton, Trump, or Machiavelli.[24]

---

[20] Chengu, Garikai. "Libya: From Africa's Wealthiest Democracy Under Gaddafi to Terrorist Haven After US Intervention." *Counterpunch*, 20 October 2015.

[21] Frank, Dana. "'She's Baldly Lying': Dana Frank Responds to Hillary Clinton's Defense of Her Role in Honduras Coup." *Democracy Now*, 13 April 2016.

[22] Cohen, Michael A. "The Day Trump Trashed US Diplomacy." *Boston Globe*, 21 July 2016.

[23] Bush, Evan. "Thinking of voting for Jill Stein or Gary Johnson? Here are their policy positions." *Seattle Times*, 28 July 2016.

[24] Hudson, John. "Exclusive: Bernie Sanders Begins Building Foreign Policy Team." *Foreign Policy*, 24 February 2016.

VI. Of New Princedoms Which a Prince Acquires with His Own Arms and by Merit

LET no man marvel if in what I am about to say concerning Princedoms wholly new, both as regards the Prince and the form of Government, I cite the highest examples. For since men for the most part follow in the footsteps and imitate the actions of others, and yet are unable to adhere exactly to those paths which others have taken, or attain to the virtues of those whom they would resemble, the wise man should always follow the roads that have been trodden by the great, and imitate those who have most excelled, so that if he cannot reach their perfection, he may at least acquire something of its savor. Acting in this like the skillful archer, who seeing that the object he would hit is distant, and knowing the range of his bow, takes aim much above the destined mark; not designing that his arrow should strike so high, but that flying high it may alight at the point intended.

I say, then, that in entirely new Princedoms where the Prince himself is new, the difficulty of maintaining possession varies with the greater or less ability of him who acquires possession. And, because the mere fact of a private person rising to be a Prince presupposes either merit or good fortune, it will be seen that the presence of one or other of these two conditions lessens, to some extent, many difficulties. And yet, he who is less beholden to Fortune has often in the end the better success; and it may be for the advantage of a Prince that, from his having no other territories, he is obliged to reside in person in the State which he has acquired.

Looking first to those who have become Princes by their merit and not by their good fortune, I say that the most excellent among them are Moses, Cyrus, Romulus, Theseus, and the like. And though perhaps I ought not to name Moses, he being merely an instrument for carrying out the Divine commands, he is still to be admired for those qualities which made him worthy to converse with God. But if we consider Cyrus and the others who have acquired or founded kingdoms, they will all be seen to be admirable. And if their actions

*and the particular institutions of which they were the authors be
studied, they will be found not to differ from those of Moses,
instructed though he was by so great a teacher. Moreover, on
examining their lives and actions, we shall see that they were
debtors to Fortune for nothing beyond the opportunity which
enabled them to shape things as they pleased, without which the
force of their spirit would have been spent in vain; as on the other
hand, opportunity would have offered itself in vain, had the capacity
for turning it to account been wanting. It was necessary, therefore,
that Moses should find the children of Israel in bondage in Egypt,
and oppressed by the Egyptians, in order that they might be
disposed to follow him, and so escape from their servitude. It was
fortunate for Romulus that he found no home in Alba, but was
exposed at the time of his birth, to the end that he might become king
and founder of the City of Rome. It was necessary that Cyrus should
find the Persians discontented with the rule of the Medes, and the
Medes enervated and effeminate from a prolonged peace. Nor could
Theseus have displayed his great qualities had he not found the
Athenians disunited and dispersed. But while it was their
opportunities that made these men fortunate, it was their own merit
that enabled them to recognize these opportunities and turn them to
account, to the glory and prosperity of their country. They who come
to the Princedom, as these did, by virtuous paths, acquire with
difficulty, but keep with ease. The difficulties which they have in
acquiring arise mainly from the new laws and institutions which
they are forced to introduce in founding and securing their
government. And let it be noted that there is no more delicate matter
to take in hand, nor more dangerous to conduct, nor more doubtful
in its success, than to set up as a leader in the introduction of
changes. For he who innovates will have for his enemies all those
who are well off under the existing order of things, and only
lukewarm supporters in those who might be better off under the new.
This lukewarm temper arises partly from the fear of adversaries who
have the laws on their side, and partly from the incredulity of
mankind, who will never admit the merit of anything new, until they
have seen it proved by the event. The result, however, is that
whenever the enemies of change make an attack, they do so with all*

the zeal of partisans, while the others defend themselves so feebly as to endanger both themselves and their cause.

But to get a clearer understanding of this part of our subject, we must look whether these innovators can stand alone, or whether they depend for aid upon others; in other words, whether to carry out their ends they must resort to entreaty, or can prevail by force. In the former case they always fare badly and bring nothing to a successful issue; but when they depend upon their own resources and can employ force, they seldom fail. Hence it comes that all armed Prophets have been victorious, and all unarmed Prophets have been destroyed.

For, besides what has been said, it should be borne in mind that the temper of the multitude is fickle, and that while it is easy to persuade them of a thing, it is hard to fix them in that persuasion. Wherefore, matters should be so ordered that when men no longer believe of their own accord, they may be compelled to believe by force. Moses, Cyrus, Theseus, and Romulus could never have made their ordinances be observed for any length of time had they been unarmed, as was the case, in our own days, with the Friar Girolamo Savonarola, whose new institutions came to nothing so soon as the multitude began to waver in their faith; since he had not the means to keep those who had been believers steadfast in their belief, or to make unbelievers believe.

Such persons, therefore, have great difficulty in carrying out their designs; but all their difficulties are on the road, and may be overcome by courage. Having conquered these, and coming to be held in reverence, and having destroyed all who were jealous of their influence, they remain powerful, safe, honored, and prosperous.

To the great examples cited above, I would add one other, of less note indeed, but assuredly bearing some proportion to them, and which may stand for all others of a like character. I mean the example of Hiero the Syracusan. He from a private station rose to

be Prince of Syracuse, and he too was indebted to Fortune only for
his opportunity. For the Syracusans being oppressed, chose him to
be their Captain, which office he so discharged as deservedly to be
made their King. For even while a private citizen his merit was so
remarkable, that one who writes of him says, he lacked nothing that
a King should have save the Kingdom. Doing away with the old
army, he organized a new, abandoned existing alliances and
assumed new allies, and with an army and allies of his own, was
able on that foundation to build what superstructure he pleased;
having trouble enough in acquiring, but none in preserving what he
had acquired.

Machiavelli advises that the wise man should "always" follow the
examples set by the "great" and, oddly, offers a final example of
Hiero and what Machiavelli describes as Hiero's "superstructure,"
anticipating Marx and Gramsci.[25] Machiavelli fails to recognize the
influence of spiritual leaders such as Confucius, Siddartha,
Muhammad, or Jesus, though Machiavelli does honor Moses as an
"instrument" of greatness, and Machiavelli clarifies that only armed
prophets meet with success. It is interesting to consider how
Machiavelli would explain such peaceful and prosperous nations as
Canada, Switzerland, Bhutan, and Costa Rica or the examples set by
Baha'u'llah, Gandhi, Betty Williams,[26] Cesar Chavez, or Nelson
Mandela.

---

[25] Preus, J. Samuel. "Machiavelli's Functional Analysis of Religion: Context and
Object." *Journal of the History of Ideas* 40, no. 2 (1979): 171-90.
[26] Young, Christine. "Utah Ulster Project Brings Northern Ireland Catholics and
Protestants Together." *Intermountain Catholic*, 29 July, 2016.

VII. Of New Princedoms Acquired by the Aid of Others and by Good Fortune

THEY who from a private station become Princes by mere good fortune, do so with little trouble, but have much trouble to maintain themselves. They meet with no hindrance on their way, being carried as it were on wings to their destination, but all their difficulties overtake them when they alight. Of this class are those on whom States are conferred either in return for money, or through the favor of him who confers them; as it happened to many in the Greek cities of Ionia and the Hellespont to be made Princes by Darius, that they might hold these cities for his security and glory; and as happened in the case of those Emperors who, from privacy, attained the Imperial dignity by corrupting the army. Such Princes are wholly dependent on the favor and fortunes of those who have made them great, which supports none could be less stable or secure; and they lack both the knowledge and the power that would enable them to maintain their position. They lack the knowledge, because unless they have great parts and force of character, it is not to be expected that having always lived in a private station they should have learned how to command. They lack the power, since they cannot look for support from attached and faithful troops. Moreover, States suddenly acquired, like all else that is produced and that grows up rapidly, can never have such root or hold as that the first storm which strikes them shall not overthrow them; unless, indeed, as I have said already, they who thus suddenly become Princes have a capacity for learning quickly how to defend what Fortune has placed in their lap, and can lay those foundations after they rise which by others are laid before.

Of each of these methods of becoming a Prince, namely, by merit and by good fortune, I shall select an instance from times within my own recollection, and shall take the cases of Francesco Sforza and Cesare Borgia. By suitable measures and singular ability, Francesco Sforza rose from privacy to be Duke of Milan, preserving with little trouble what it cost him infinite efforts to gain. On the other hand, Cesare Borgia, vulgarly spoken of as Duke Valentino, obtained his Princedom through the favorable fortunes of his father, and with these lost it, although, so far as in him lay, he used every effort and practiced every expedient that a prudent and able man should, who desires to strike root in a State given him by the arms and fortune of another. For, as I have already said, he who does not lay his foundations at first, may, if he be of great parts, succeed in laying them afterwards, though with inconvenience to the builder and risk to the building. And if we consider the various measures taken by Duke Valentino, we shall perceive how broad were the foundations he had laid whereon to rest his future power. These I think it not superfluous to examine, since I know not what lessons I could teach a new Prince, more useful than the example of his actions. And if the measures taken by him did not profit him in the end, it was through no fault of his, but from the extraordinary and extreme malignity of Fortune.

In his efforts to aggrandize the Duke his son, Alexander VI had to face many difficulties, both immediate and remote. In the first place, he saw no way to make him Lord of any State which was not a State of the Church, while, if he sought to take for him a State belonging to the Church, he knew that the Duke of Milan and the Venetians would withhold their consent; Faenza and Rimini being already under the protection of the latter. Further, he saw that the arms of Italy, and those more especially of which he might have availed himself, were in the hands of men who had reason to fear his aggrandizement, that is, of the Orsini, the Colonnesi, and their followers. These therefore he could not trust. It was consequently necessary that the existing order of things should be changed, and the States of Italy thrown into confusion, in order that he might safely make himself master of some part of them; and this became easy for him when he found that the Venetians, moved by other causes, were plotting to bring the French once more into Italy. This design he accordingly did not oppose, but furthered by annulling the first marriage of the French King.

King Louis therefore came into Italy at the instance of the Venetians, and with the consent of Pope Alexander, and no sooner was he in Milan than the Pope got troops from him to aid him in his enterprise against Romagna, which Province, moved by the reputation of the French arms, at once submitted. After thus obtaining possession of Romagna, and after quelling the Colonnesi, Duke Valentino was desirous to follow up and extend his conquests. Two causes, however, held him back, namely, the doubtful fidelity of his own forces, and the waywardness of France. For he feared that the Orsini, of whose arms he had made use, might fail him, and not merely prove a hindrance to further acquisitions, but take from him what he had gained, and that the King might serve him the same turn. How little he could count on the Orsini was made plain when, after the capture of Faenza, he turned his arms against Bologna, and saw how reluctantly they took part in that enterprise. The King's mind he understood, when, after seizing on the Dukedom of Urbino, he was about to attack Tuscany; from which design Louis compelled him to desist. Whereupon the Duke resolved to depend no longer on the arms or fortune of others. His first step, therefore, was to weaken the factions of the Orsini and Colonnesi in Rome. Those of their following who were of good birth, he gained over by making them his own gentlemen, assigning them a liberal provision, and conferring upon them commands and appointments suited to their rank; so that in a few months their old partisan attachments died out, and the hopes of all rested on the Duke alone.

He then awaited an occasion to crush the chiefs of the Orsini, for those of the house of Colonna he had already scattered, and a good opportunity presenting itself, he turned it to the best account. For when the Orsini came at last to see that the greatness of the Duke and the Church involved their ruin, they assembled a council at Magione in the Perugian territory, whence resulted the revolt of Urbino, commotions in Romagna, and an infinity of dangers to the Duke, all of which he overcame with the help of France. His credit thus restored, the Duke trusting no longer either to the French or to any other foreign aid, that he might not have to confront them openly, resorted to stratagem, and was so well able to dissemble his designs, that the Orsini, through the mediation of Signor Paolo (whom he failed not to secure by every friendly attention, furnishing him with clothes, money, and horses), were so won over as to be drawn in their simplicity into his hands at Sinigaglia. When the leaders were thus disposed of, and their followers made his friends, the Duke had laid sufficiently good foundations for his future power, since he held all Romagna together with the Dukedom of Urbino, and had ingratiated himself with the entire population of these States, who now began to see that they were well off. And since this part of his conduct merits both attention and imitation, I shall not pass it over in silence. After the Duke had taken Romagna, finding that it had been ruled by feeble Lords, who thought more of plundering than correcting their subjects, and gave them more cause for division than for union, so that the country was overrun with robbery, tumult, and every kind of outrage, he judged it necessary, with a view to render it peaceful and obedient to his authority, to provide it with a good government. Accordingly, he set over it Messer Remiro d'Orco, a stern and prompt ruler, who being entrusted with the fullest powers, in a very short time, and with much credit to himself, restored it to tranquility and order. But afterwards apprehending that such unlimited authority might become odious, the Duke decided that it was no longer needed, and established in the center of the Province a civil Tribunal, with an excellent President, in which every town was represented by its advocate. And knowing that past severities had generated ill-feeling against himself, in order to purge the minds of the people and gain their good-will, he sought to show them that any cruelty which had been done had not originated, with him, but in the harsh disposition of his minister. Availing himself of the pretext which this afforded, he one morning caused Remiro to be beheaded, and exposed in the market place of Cesena with a block and bloody axe by his side. The barbarity of which spectacle at once astounded and satisfied the populace.

But, returning to the point whence we diverged, I say that the Duke, finding himself fairly strong and in a measure secured against present dangers, being furnished with arms of his own choosing and having to a great extent got rid of those which, if left near him, might have caused him trouble, had to consider, if he desired to follow up his conquests, how he was to deal with France, since he saw he could expect no further support from King Louis, whose eyes were at last opened to his mistake. He therefore began to look about for new alliances, and to waver in his adherence to the French, then occupied with their expedition into the kingdom of Naples against the Spaniards, at that time laying siege to Gaeta; his object being to secure himself against France; and in this he would soon have succeeded had Alexander lived.

Such was the line he took to meet present exigencies. As regards the future, he had to apprehend that a new Head of the Church might not be his friend, and might even seek to deprive him of what Alexander had given. This he thought to provide against in four ways. First, by exterminating all who were of kin to those Lords whom he had despoiled of their possessions, that they might not become instruments in the hands of a new Pope. Second, by gaining over all the Roman nobles, so as to be able with their help to put a bridle, as the saying is, in the Pope's mouth. Third, by bringing the college of Cardinals, so far as he could, under his control. And fourth, by establishing his authority so firmly before his father's death, as to be able by himself to withstand the shock of a first onset.

Of these measures, at the time when Alexander died, he had already effected three, and had almost carried out the forth. For of the Lords whose possessions he had usurped, he had put to death all whom he could reach, and very few had escaped. He had gained over the Roman nobility, and had the majority in the College of Cardinals on his side.

As to further acquisitions, his design was to make himself master of Tuscany. He was already in possession of Perugia and Piombino, and had assumed the protectorate of Pisa, on which city he was about to spring; taking no heed of France, as indeed he no longer had occasion, since the French had been deprived of the kingdom of Naples by the Spaniards under circumstances which made it necessary for both nations to buy his friendship. Pisa taken, Lucca and Siena would soon have yielded, partly through jealousy of

Florence, partly through fear, and the position of the Florentines must then have been desperate.

Had he therefore succeeded in these designs, as he was succeeding in that very year in which Alexander died, he would have won such power and reputation that he might afterwards have stood alone, relying on his own strength and resources, without being beholden to the power and fortune of others. But Alexander died five years from the time he first unsheathed the sword, leaving his son with the State of Romagna alone consolidated, with all the rest unsettled, between two powerful hostile armies, and sick almost to death. And yet such were the fire and courage of the Duke, he knew so well how men must either be conciliated or crushed, and so solid were the foundations he had laid in that brief period, that had these armies not been upon his back, or had he been in sound health, he must have surmounted every difficulty.

How strong his foundations were may be seen from this, that Romagna waited for him for more than a month; and that although half dead, he remained in safety in Rome, where though the Baglioni, the Vitelli, and the Orsini came to attack him, they met with no success. Moreover, since he was able if not to make whom he liked Pope, at least to prevent the election of any whom he disliked, had he been in health at the time when Alexander died, all would have been easy for him. But he told me himself on the day on which Julius II was created, that he had foreseen and provided for everything else that could happen on his father's death, but had never anticipated that when his father died he too should be at death's-door.

Taking all these actions of the Duke together, I can find no fault with him; nay, it seems to me reasonable to put him forward, as I have done, as a pattern for all such as rise to power by good fortune and the help of others. For with his great spirit and high aims he could not act otherwise than he did, and nothing but the shortness of his father's life and his own illness prevented the success of his designs. Whoever, therefore, on entering a new Princedom, judges it necessary to rid himself of enemies, to conciliate friends, to prevail by force or fraud, to make himself feared yet not hated by his subjects, respected and obeyed by his soldiers, to crush those who can or ought to injure him, to introduce changes in the old order of things, to be at once severe and affable, magnanimous and liberal, to do away with a mutinous army and create a new one, to maintain relations with Kings and Princes on such a footing that they must see it for their interest to aid him, and dangerous to offend, can find no brighter example than in the actions of this Prince.

The one thing for which he may be blamed was the creation of Pope Julius II, in respect of whom he chose badly. Because, as I have said already, though he could not secure the election he desired, he could have prevented any other; and he ought never to have consented to the creation of any one of those Cardinals whom he had injured, or who on becoming Pope would have reason to fear him; for fear is as dangerous an enemy as resentment. Those whom he had offended were, among others, San Pietro ad Vincula, Colonna, San Giorgio, and Ascanio; all the rest, excepting d'Amboise and the Spanish Cardinals (the latter from their connection and obligations, the former from the power he derived through his relations with the French Court), would on assuming the Pontificate have had reason to fear him. The duke, therefore, ought, in the first place, to have labored for the creation of a Spanish Pope; failing in which, he should have agreed to the election of d'Amboise, but never to that of San Pietro ad Vincula. And he deceives himself who believes that with the great, recent benefits cause old wrongs to be forgotten. The Duke, therefore, erred in the part he took in this election; and his error was the cause of his ultimate downfall.

It is interesting to consider Trump's inheritance[27] and candidacy in light of Machiavelli's opening claim in this chapter that those "who from a private station become Princes by mere good fortune, do so with little trouble, but have much trouble to maintain themselves."

---

[27] Swanson, Ana. "The Myth and the Reality of Donald Trump's Business Empire." *Washington Post*, 29 February 2016.

Machiavelli, more eerily, foreshadows his own ultimate fate by mentioning the torture of Messer Remiro d'Orco.[28]

---

[28] Smith, Steven. "Introduction to Political Philosophy: Lecture 10 Transcript. *Yale University,*

VIII. Of Those Who by Their Crimes Come to Be Princes

BUT since from privacy a man may also rise to be a Prince in one or other of two ways, neither of which can be referred wholly either to merit or to fortune, it is fit that I notice them here, though one of them may fall to be discussed more fully in treating of Republics.

The ways I speak of are, first, when the ascent to power is made by paths of wickedness and crime; and second, when a private person becomes ruler of his country by the favor of his fellow-citizens. The former method I shall make clear by two examples, one ancient, the other modern, without entering further into the merits of the matter, for these, I think, should be enough for anyone who is driven to follow them.

Agathocles the Sicilian came, not merely from a private station, but from the very dregs of the people, to be King of Syracuse. Son of a potter, through all the stages of his fortunes he led a foul life. His vices, however, were conjoined with so great vigor both of mind and body, that becoming a soldier, he rose through the various grades of the service to be Praetor of Syracuse. Once established in that post, he resolved to make himself Prince, and to hold by violence and without obligation to others the authority which had been spontaneously entrusted to him. Accordingly, after imparting his design to Hamilcar, who with the Carthaginian armies was at that time waging war in Sicily, he one morning assembled the people and senate of Syracuse as though to consult with them on matters of public moment, and on a pre-concerted signal caused his soldiers to put to death all the senators, and the wealthiest of the commons. These being thus got rid of, he assumed and retained possession of the sovereignty without opposition on the part of the people; and although twice defeated by the Carthaginians, and afterwards besieged, he was able not only to defend his city, but leaving a part of his forces for its protection, to invade Africa with the remainder, and so in a short time to raise the siege of Syracuse, reducing the Carthaginians to the utmost extremities, and compelling them to make terms whereby they abandoned Sicily to him and confined themselves to Africa.

Whoever examines this man's actions and achievements will discover little or nothing in them which can be ascribed to Fortune, seeing, as has already been said, that it was not through the favor of any, but by the regular steps of the military service, gained at the cost of a thousand hardships and hazards, he reached the princedom which he afterwards maintained by so many daring and dangerous enterprises. Still, to slaughter fellow citizens, to betray friends, to be devoid of honor, pity, and religion, cannot be counted as merits, for these are means which may lead to power, but which confer no glory. Wherefore, if in respect of the valor with which he encountered and extricated himself from difficulties, and the constancy of his spirit in supporting and conquering adverse fortune, there seems no reason to judge him inferior to the greatest captains that have ever lived, his unbridled cruelty and inhumanity, together with his countless crimes, forbid us to number him with the greatest men; but, at any rate, we cannot attribute to Fortune or to merit what he accomplished without either. In our own times, during the papacy of Alexander VI, Oliverotto of Fermo, who some years before had been left an orphan, and had been brought up by his maternal uncle Giovanni Fogliani, was sent while still a lad to serve under Paolo Vitelli, in the expectation that a thorough training under that commander might qualify him for high rank as a soldier. After the death of Paolo, he served under his brother Vitellozzo, and in a very short time, being of a quick wit, hardy and resolute, he became one of the first soldiers of his company. But thinking it beneath him to serve under others, with the countenance of the Vitelleschi and the connivance of certain citizens of Fermo who preferred the slavery to the freedom of their country, he formed the design to seize on that town.

He accordingly wrote to Giovanni Fogliani that after many years of absence from home, he desired to see him and his native city once more, and to look a little into the condition of his patrimony; and as his one endeavor had been to make himself a name, in order that his fellow-citizens might see his time had not been misspent, he proposed to return honorably attended by a hundred horsemen from among his own friends and followers; and he begged Giovanni graciously to arrange for his reception by the citizens of Fermo with corresponding marks of distinction, as this would be creditable not only to himself, but also to the uncle who had brought him up.

Giovanni, accordingly, did not fail in any proper attention to his nephew, but caused him to be splendidly received by his fellow-citizens, and lodged him in his house; where Oliverotto having passed some days, and made the necessary arrangements for carrying out his wickedness, gave a formal banquet, to which he invited his uncle and all the first men of Fermo. When the repast and the other entertainments proper to such an occasion had come to an end, Oliverotto artfully turned the conversation to matters of grave interest, by speaking of the greatness of Pope Alexander and Cesare his son, and of their enterprises; and when Giovanni and the others were replying to what he said, he suddenly rose up, observing that these were matters to be discussed in a more private place, and so withdrew to another chamber; whither his uncle and all the other citizens followed him, and where they had no sooner seated themselves, than soldiers rushing out from places of concealment put Giovanni and all the rest to death.

After this butchery, Oliverotto mounted his horse, rode through the streets, and besieged the chief magistrate in the palace, so that all were constrained by fear to yield obedience and accept a government of which he made himself the head. And all who from being disaffected were likely to stand in his way, he put to death, while he strengthened himself with new ordinances, civil and military, to such purpose, that for the space of a year during which he retained the Princedom, he not merely kept a firm hold of the city, but grew formidable to all his neighbors. And it would have been as impossible to unseat him as it was to unseat Agathocles, had he not let himself be overreached by Cesare Borgia on the occasion when, as has already been told, the Orsini and Vitelli were entrapped at Sinigaglia; where he too being taken, one year after the commission of his parricidal crime, was strangled along with Vitellozzo, whom he had assumed for his master in villainy as in valor. It may be asked how Agathocles and some like him, after numberless acts of treachery and cruelty, have been able to live long in their own country in safety, and to defend themselves from foreign enemies, without being plotted against by their fellow-citizens, whereas, many others, by reason of their cruelty, have failed to maintain their position even in peaceful times, not to speak of the perilous times of war. I believe that this results from cruelty being well or ill-employed. Those cruelties we may say are well employed, if it be permitted to speak well of things evil, which are done once for all under the necessity of self-preservation, and are not afterwards persisted in, but so far as possible modified to the advantage of the governed. Ill-employed cruelties, on the other hand, are those which from small beginnings increase rather than diminish with time. They who follow the first of these methods, may, by the grace of God and man, find, as did Agathocles, that their condition is not desperate; but by no possibility can the others maintain themselves.

Hence we may learn the lesson that on seizing a state, the usurper should make haste to inflict what injuries he must, at a stroke, that he may not have to renew them daily, but be enabled by their discontinuance to reassure men's minds, and afterwards win them over by benefits. Whosoever, either through timidity or from following bad counsels, adopts a contrary course, must keep the sword always drawn, and can put no trust in his subjects, who suffering from continued and constantly renewed severities, will never yield him their confidence. Injuries, therefore, should be inflicted all at once, that their ill savor being less lasting may the less offend; whereas, benefits should be conferred little by little, that so they may be more fully relished.

But, before all things, a Prince should so live with his subjects that no vicissitude of good or evil fortune shall oblige him to alter his behavior; because, if a need to change come through adversity, it is then too late to resort to severity; while any leniency you may use will be thrown away, for it will be seen to be compulsory and gain you no thanks.

Machiavelli mentions governance other than monarchy for the first time here: "Republics." But, he only mentions the option to disregard it. Machiavelli's advice not to alter behavior regardless of good or evil fortune seems to be as widely and deeply practiced in the current "double-down" or "triple-down" stubbornness of Republicans and Trump in particular—especially in his response to insulted the Khan family, whose son earned a Bronze Star for valor in Iraq.[29] Since most modern politicians are wealthy, their fortunes do not rise and fall with voters, so Clinton and Trump feign empathy.[30] General Colin Powell clearly borrowed his own "decisive victory" doctrine[31] from Machiavelli's advice that "Injuries, therefore, should be inflicted all at once, that their ill savor being less lasting may the less offend." The example of Agathocles should duly frighten us all; Hitler's minions only set fire to the Riechstag,[32] but Agathocles slaughtered the senators and wealthiest citizens.[33] Yet, for all the carnage, Agathocles repeatedly failed in his foreign adventures, and he died in defeat and shame. Sanders consistently counsels restraint.[34] Johnson, on the other hand, offers a less ruthless governance,[35] and Stein even less ruthless still.

---

[29] "Trump Slated Over 'Insult' to Dead Soldier's Parents." *AlJazeera*, 1 August 2016.

[30] Martosko, David. "Road to the White House? *Daily Mail*, 12 April 2015.

[31] Walt, Stephen. "Applying the 8 Questions of the Powell Doctrine to Syria." *Foreign Policy*, 3 September 2013.

[32] Ferguson, Thomas, and Voth Hans-Joachim. "Betting on Hitler: The Value of Political Connections in Nazi Germany." *The Quarterly Journal of Economics* 123, no. 1 (2008): 101-37.

[33] Lewis, Sian. "Tyrants and Kings." In *Greek Tyranny*, 102-21. Liverpool University Press, 2009.

[34] Ponnuru, Ramesh. "Why the Democrats Can Move to the Left." *Bloomberg View*, 13 July 2016.

[35] Shane, Leo III. "Libertarian Hopeful Argues for Smaller Military, Less Foreign Intervention." *Military Times*, 22 June 2016.

IX. Of the Civil Princedom

I COME now to the second case, namely, of the leading citizen who, not by crimes or violence, but by the favor of his fellow-citizens is made Prince of his country. This may be called a Civil Princedom, and its attainment depends not wholly on merit, nor wholly on good fortune, but rather on what may be termed a fortunate astuteness. I say then that the road to this Princedom lies either through the favor of the people or of the nobles. For in every city are to be found these two opposed humors having their origin in this, that the people desire not to be domineered over or oppressed by the nobles, while the nobles desire to oppress and domineer over the people. And from these two contrary appetites there arises in cities one of three results, a Princedom, or Liberty, or License. A Princedom is created either by the people or by the nobles, according as one or other of these factions has occasion for it. For when the nobles perceive that they cannot withstand the people, they set to work to magnify the reputation of one of their number, and make him their Prince, to the end that under his shadow they may be enabled to indulge their desires. The people, on the other hand, when they see that they cannot make head against the nobles, invest a single citizen with all their influence and make him Prince, that they may have the shelter of his authority. He who is made Prince by the favor of the nobles, has greater difficulty to maintain himself than he who comes to the Princedom by aid of the people, since he finds many about him who think themselves as good as he, and whom, on that account, he cannot guide or govern as he would. But he who reaches the Princedom by the popular support, finds himself alone, with none, or but a very few about him who are not ready to obey. Moreover, the demands of the nobles cannot be satisfied with credit to the Prince, nor without injury to others, while those of the people well may, the aim of the people being more honorable than that of the nobles, the latter seeking to oppress, the former not to be oppressed. Add to this, that a Prince can never secure himself against a disaffected people, their number being too great, while he may against a disaffected nobility, since their number is small. The worst that a Prince need fear from a disaffected people is, that they may desert him, whereas when the nobles are his enemies he has to fear not only that they may desert him, but also that they may turn against him; because, as they have greater craft and foresight, they always choose their time to suit their safety, and seek favor with the side they think will win. Again, a Prince must always live with the same people, but need not always live with the same nobles, being able to make and unmake these from day to day, and give and take away their authority at his pleasure.

But to make this part of the matter clearer, I say that as regards the nobles there is this first distinction to be made. They either so govern their conduct as to bind themselves wholly to your fortunes, or they do not. Those who so bind themselves, and who are not grasping, should be loved and honored. As to those who do not so bind themselves, there is this further distinction. For the most part they are held back by pusillanimity and a natural defect of courage, in which case you should make use of them, and of those among them more especially who are prudent, for they will do you honor in prosperity, and in adversity give you no cause for fear. But where they abstain from attaching themselves to you of set purpose and for ambitious ends, it is a sign that they are thinking more of themselves than of you, and against such men a Prince should be on his guard, and treat them as though they were declared enemies, for in his adversity they will always help to ruin him.

He who becomes a Prince through the favor of the people should always keep on good terms with them; which it is easy for him to do, since all they ask is not to be oppressed. But he who against the will of the people is made a Prince by the favor of the nobles, must, above all things, seek to conciliate the people, which he readily may by taking them under his protection. For since men who are well treated by one whom they expected to treat them ill, feel the more beholden to their benefactor, the people will at once become better disposed to such a Prince when he protects them, than if he owed his Princedom to them. 4 There are many ways in which a Prince may gain the good-will of the people, but, because these vary with circumstances, no certain rule can be laid down respecting them, and

I shall, therefore, say no more about them. But this is the sum of the matter, that it is essential for a Prince to be on a friendly footing with his people, since otherwise, he will have no resource in adversity. Nabis, Prince of Sparta, was attacked by the whole hosts of Greece, and by a Roman army flushed with victory, and defended his country and crown against them; and when danger approached, there were but few of his subjects against whom he needed to guard himself, whereas had the people been hostile, this would not have been enough. And what I affirm let no one controvert by citing the old saw that 'he who builds on the people builds on mire,' for that may be true of a private citizen who presumes on his favor with the people, and counts on being rescued by them when overpowered by his enemies or by the magistrates. In such cases a man may often find himself deceived, as happened to the Gracchi in Rome, and in Florence to Messer Giorgio Scali. But when he who builds on the people is a Prince capable of command, of a spirit not to be cast down by ill-fortune, who, while he animates the whole community by his courage and bearing, neglects no prudent precaution, he will not find himself betrayed by the people, but will be seen to have laid his foundations well.

The most critical juncture for Princedoms of this kind, is at the moment when they are about to pass from the popular to the absolute form of government: and as these Princes exercise their authority either directly or through the agency of the magistrates, in the latter case their position is weaker and more hazardous, since they are wholly in the power of those citizens to whom the magistracies are entrusted, who can, and especially in difficult times, with the greatest ease deprive them of their authority, either by opposing, or by not obeying them. And in times of peril it is too late for a Prince to assume to himself an absolute authority, for the citizens and subjects who are accustomed to take their orders from the magistrates, will not when dangers threaten take them from the Prince, so that at such seasons there will always be very few in whom he can trust. Such Princes, therefore, must not build on what they see in tranquil times when the citizens feel the need of the State. For then everyone is ready to run, to promise, and, danger of death being remote, even to die for the State. But in troubled times, when the State has need of its citizens, few of them are to be found. And the risk of the experiment is the greater in that it can only be made once. Wherefore, a wise Prince should devise means whereby his subjects may at all times, whether favorable or adverse, feel the need of the State and of him, and then they will always be faithful to him.

Machiavelli seems to anticipate Stein in advising that "He who is made Prince by the favor of the nobles, has greater difficulty to maintain himself than he who comes to the Princedom by aid of the people, since he finds many about him who think themselves as good as he, and whom, on that account, he cannot guide or govern as he would." Yet Stein purposefully speaks in first person plural, not singular.[36] Johnson, polling at 13% in August 2016, seems to echo Machiavelli's populist admonition that "a Prince can never secure himself against a disaffected people, their number being too great, while he may against a disaffected nobility, since their number is small." But, can Johnson garner enough coverage from media nobility to share his message?[37] Trump, though, shows the currency of Machiavelli's claim that "a Prince must always live with the same people, but need not always live with the same nobles, being able to make and unmake these from day to day, and give and take away their authority at his pleasure." As such, Trump continues to throw bloody red meat to his base, regardless of criticism from party elites.[38] And Clinton worries, as Machiavelli warns, that "a disaffected people…may desert." Nonwhites, in fact, seem to like Clinton less the more she campaigns.[39] Whereas, Sanders chose to learn at the Democratic National Convention that "as regards the nobles….they are held back by pusillanimity and a

[36] Stein, Jill. "We Broke the Internet." *Jill2016*, 19 July 2016.
[37] "Blackout CNN for Gary Johnson." *Gary Johnson Grassroots Blog*, 15 July 2012.
[38] Hayden, Michael Edison. "Trump Calls Capt. Khan a 'Hero' Amid Blowback Over Remarks to Family." *ABC News*, 1 August 2016.
[39] Abramson, Seth. "Hillary Clinton's Support of Nonwhite Voters Has Collapsed." *Huffington Post*, 31 March 2016.

natural defect of courage…where they abstain from attaching themselves to you of set purpose and for ambitious ends, it is a sign that they are thinking more of themselves than of you, and against such men a Prince should be on his guard, and treat them as though they were declared enemies." Nevertheless, Sanders endorsed Clinton soon after he complained of widespread party corruption and party election irregularities.[40] So, isn't this politics-as-usual a Machiavellian suicide pact?

---

[40] Foran, Clare. "Is the Democratic Primary Really Rigged?" *The Atlantic*, 16 May 2016.

X. How the Strength of All Princedoms Should Be Measured

IN examining the character of these Princedoms, another circumstance has to be considered, namely, whether the Prince is strong enough, if occasion demands, to stand alone, or whether he needs continual help from others. To make the matter clearer, I pronounce those to be able to stand alone who, with the men and money at their disposal, can get together an army fit to take the field against any assailant; and, conversely, I judge those to be in constant need of help who cannot take the field against their enemies, but are obliged to retire behind their walls, and to defend themselves there. Of the former I have already spoken, and shall speak again as occasion may require. As to the latter there is nothing to be said, except to exhort such Princes to strengthen and fortify the towns in which they dwell, and take no heed of the country outside. For whoever has thoroughly fortified his town, and put himself on such a footing with his subjects as I have already indicated and shall hereafter speak of, will always be attacked with much circumspection; for men are always averse to enterprises that are attended with difficulty, and it is impossible not to foresee difficulties in attacking a Prince whose town is strongly fortified and who is not hated by his subjects. The towns of Germany enjoy great freedom. Having little territory, they render obedience to the Emperor only when so disposed, fearing neither him nor any other neighboring power. For they are so fortified that it is plain to everyone that it would be a tedious and difficult task to reduce them, since all of them are protected by moats and suitable ramparts, are well supplied with artillery, and keep their public magazines constantly stored with victual, drink and fuel, enough to last them for a year. Besides which, in order to support the poorer class of citizens without public loss, they lay in a common stock of materials for these to work on for a year, in the handicrafts which are the life and sinews of such cities, and by which the common people live. Moreover, they esteem military exercises and have many regulations for their maintenance.

A Prince, therefore, who has a strong city, and who does not make himself hated, cannot be attacked, or should he be so, his assailant will come badly off; since human affairs are so variable that it is almost impossible for anyone to keep an army posted in leaguer for a whole year without interruption of some sort. Should it be objected that if the citizens have possessions outside the town, and see them burned, they will lose patience, and that self-interest, together with the hardships of a protracted siege, will cause them to forget their loyalty; I answer that a capable and courageous Prince will always overcome these difficulties, now, by holding out hopes to his subjects that the evil will not be of long continuance; now, by exciting their fears of the enemy's cruelty; and, again, by dexterously silencing those who seem to him too forward in their complaints. Moreover, it is to be expected that the enemy will burn and lay waste the country immediately on their arrival, at a time when men's minds are still heated and resolute for defense. And for this very reason the Prince ought the less to fear, because after a few days, when the first ardor has abated, the injury is already done and suffered, and cannot be undone; and the people will now, all the more readily, make common cause with their Prince from his seeming to be under obligations to them, their houses having been burned and their lands wasted in his defense. For it is the nature of men to incur obligation as much by the benefits they render as by those they receive.

Wherefore, if the whole matter be well considered, it ought not to be difficult for a prudent Prince, both at the outset and afterwards, to maintain the spirits of his subjects during a siege; provided always that victuals and other means of defense do not run short.

Machiavelli's proposal that Prince lead on his own would seem as outdated as foolish, until the spectacle of the 2016 Republican National Convention. Not only did Trump promise to solve pressing problems himself, many delegates urged him to do so and the rest of follow or step aside.[41] Even the warmongering darling of Wall

---

[41] Applebaum, Yoni. "I Alone Can Fix It." *The Atlantic*, 21 July 2016.

Street Clinton has been savvy enough to invite collaboration, especially with Sanders and his many supporters.[42] Machiavelli sees adequate food and supplies as the only obstacles for a Prince to maintain support during a siege, but this approach led to widespread desertion of Iraqi forces, many of whom looted on their way out of Mosul, in the face of ISIS.[43] The repeated "exciting their fears of the enemy's cruelty" did not persuade the Iraqi forces to fight harder, as Machiavelli predicts, but only gave them more cause to flee. Stein's solution is based on her assessment that the "War on Terror…has only created more terror," and "the creation of ISIS…has been an utter, unmitigated disaster, and the massive refugee crisis which is threatening to tear apart the European Union." Stein further proposes radical reforms preventing military and other government contractors from "buying their way into policy: If you establish that anyone who contributes, who provides campaign contributions, or who lobbies is not eligible for contracting with the government."[44]

---

[42] Swan, Jonathan. "Clinton Adds $27 Donate Option to Woo Sanders Supporters." *The Hill*, 12 July 2016.
[43] Ditz, Jason. "Iraq's Offensive near Mosul Collapsing in the Face of Mass Desertions." *AntiWar*, 29 March 2016.
[44] Swanson, David. "Stein's Platform More Viable than Sanders'." *American Herald Tribune*, 29 January 2016.

XI. Of Ecclesiastical Princedoms

IT now only remains for me to treat of Ecclesiastical Princedoms, all the difficulties in respect of which precede their acquisition. For they are acquired by merit or good fortune, but are maintained without either; being upheld by the venerable ordinances of Religion, which are all of such a nature and efficacy that they secure the authority of their Princes in whatever way they may act or live. These Princes alone have territories which they do not defend, and subjects whom they do not govern; yet their territories are not taken from them through not being defended, nor are their subjects concerned at not being governed, or led to think of throwing off their allegiance; nor is it in their power to do so. Accordingly, these Princedoms alone are secure and happy. But inasmuch as they are sustained by agencies of a higher nature than the mind of man can reach, I forbear to speak of them: for since they are set up and supported by God himself, he would be a rash and presumptuous man who should venture to discuss them. Nevertheless, should any one ask me how it comes about that the temporal power of the Church, which before the time of Alexander was looked on with contempt by all the Potentates of Italy, and not only by those so styling themselves, but by every Baron and Lordling however insignificant, has now reached such a pitch of greatness that the King of France trembles before it, and that it has been able to drive him out of Italy and to crush the Venetians; though the causes be known, it seems to me not superfluous to call them in some measure to recollection.

Before Charles of France passed into Italy, that country was under the control of the Pope, the Venetians, the King of Naples, the Duke of Milan, and the Florentines. Two chief objects had to be kept in view by all these powers: first, that no armed foreigner should be allowed to invade Italy; second, that no one of their own number should be suffered to extend his territory. Those whom it was especially needed to guard against, were the Pope and the Venetians. To hold back the Venetians it was necessary that all the other States should combine, as was done for the defense of

Ferrara; while to restrain the Pope, use was made of the Roman Barons, who being divided into two factions, the Orsini and Colonnesi, had constant cause for feud with one another, and standing with arms in their hands under the very eyes of the Pontiff, kept the Popedom feeble and insecure.

And although there arose from time to time a courageous Pope like Sixtus, neither his prudence nor his good fortune could free him from these embarrassments. The cause whereof was the shortness of the lives of the Popes. For in the ten years, which was the average duration of a Pope's life, he could barely succeed in humbling one of these factions; so that if, for instance, one Pope had almost exterminated the Colonnesi, he was followed by another, who being the enemy of the Orsini had no time to rid himself of them, but so far from completing the destruction of the Colonnesi, restored them to life. This led to the temporal authority of the Popes being little esteemed in Italy.

Then came Alexander VI, who more than any of his predecessors showed what a Pope could effect with money and arms, achieving by the instrumentality of Duke Valentino, and by taking advantage of the coming of the French into Italy, all those successes which I have already noticed in speaking of the actions of the Duke. And although his object was to aggrandize, not the Church but the Duke, what he did turned to the advantage of the Church, which after his death, and after the Duke had been put out of the way, became the heir of his labors.

After him came Pope Julius, who found the Church strengthened by the possession of the whole of Romagna, and the Roman Barons exhausted and their factions shattered under the blows of Pope Alexander. He found also a way opened for the accumulation of wealth, which before the time of Alexander no one had followed. These advantages Julius not only used but added to. He undertook the conquest of Bologna, the overthrow of the Venetians, and the expulsion of the French from Italy; in all which enterprises he succeeded, and with the greater glory to himself in that whatever he did, was done to strengthen the Church and not to aggrandize any private person. He succeeded, moreover, in keeping the factions of the Orsini and Colonnesi within the same limits as he found them; and, though some seeds of insubordination may still have been left among them, two causes operated to hold them in check; first, the great power of the Church, which overawed them, and second, their being without Cardinals, who had been the cause of all their disorders. For these factions while they have Cardinals among them can never be at rest, since it is they who foment dissension both in Rome and out of it, in which the Barons are forced to take part, the ambition of the Prelates thus giving rise to tumult and discord among the Barons. His Holiness, Pope Leo, has consequently found the Papacy most powerful; and from him we may hope, that as his predecessors made it great with arms, he will render it still greater and more venerable by his benignity and other countless virtues.

Machiavelli fails to address the long peace tradition of all major religions;[45] he further fails to predict the deconstruction of the Roman Catholic Church due to the worldwide child rape prosecutions of ordained clergy, long hidden by the Vatican.[46] It is interesting to consider, however, Machiavelli's observation that "inasmuch as [Ecclesiastical Princes] are sustained by agencies of a higher nature than the mind of man can reach…he would be a rash and presumptuous man who should venture to discuss them," in light of the notion of American Exceptionalism, which finds much support among evangelicals.[47] The arguably un-Christian Trump enjoys much support from the evangelicals, but mainly for his position on abortion and promise to nominate Supreme Court justices of similar beliefs to Scalia.[48] And, more to the point, most

---

[45] Szalewski, Susan. "At Omaha Prayer service, a Call for Peace and Unity in Face of Tragedies." *Omaha World-Herald*, 31 July 2016.

[46] Gledhill, Ruth. "New Vatican Role for US Archbishop Signals Move to a More Moderate Church." *Christian Today*, 8 July 2016.

[47] Baker, Douglass E. "Does American Exceptionalism Mean Worshipping the State?" The Federalist, 20 February 2016.

[48] Kapur, Sahil. "Trump Errors Stymie Effort to Use Supreme Court to Rally

Americans would not agree with the absurd idea that Trump as leader is above not only criticism but even discussion, though Trump often disregards freedom of speech so blatantly.[49] Moreover, the role of organized religion and leaders, and especially Western politics, is on the wane.[50] Some have gone as far as to describe an "exit from religion,"[51] which Machiavelli does not seem to be able to imagine. Clinton supporters, however, considered smearing Sanders as an atheist so as to gain Southern Christian voters.[52] Johnson and Stein, though, support separation of church and state.

Conservatives." *Bloomberg*, July 2016.

[49] "Trump Wants to Weaken Libel Laws Amid Feuds with Reporters." *Fox News*, 27 February 2016.

[50] Jones, Benjamin. "Is it any Wonder Religion is on the Wane?" *The Guardian*, 12 February 2015.

[51] Gauchet, Marcel. "The Disenchantment of the World." Trans. Oscar Burge. Princeton: Princeton University Press, 1997.

[52] Buncombe, Andrew. "Bernie Sanders 'Furious' over Democratic Party Plot to Smear Him as an Athiest." *Independent*, 24 July 2016.

XII. How Many Different Kinds of Soldiers There Are, and of Mercenaries

HAVING spoken particularly of all the various kinds of Princedom whereof at the outset I proposed to treat, considered in some measure what are the causes of their strength and weakness, and pointed out the methods by which men commonly seek to acquire them, it now remains that I should discourse generally concerning the means for attack and defense of which each of these different kinds of Princedom may make use.

I have already said that a Prince must lay solid foundations, since otherwise he will inevitably be destroyed. Now the main foundations of all States, whether new, old, or mixed, are good laws and good arms. But since you cannot have the former without the latter, and where you have the latter, are likely to have the former, I shall here omit all discussion on the subject of laws, and speak only of arms.

I say then that the arms wherewith a Prince defends his State are either his own subjects, or they are mercenaries, or they are auxiliaries, or they are partly one and partly another. Mercenaries and auxiliaries are at once useless and dangerous, and he who holds his State by means of mercenary troops can never be solidly or securely seated. For such troops are disunited, ambitious, insubordinate, treacherous, insolent among friends, cowardly before foes, and without fear of God or faith with man. Whenever they are attacked defeat follows; so that in peace you are plundered by them, in war by your enemies. And this because they have no tie or motive to keep them in the field beyond their paltry pay, in return for which it would be too much to expect them to give their lives. They are ready enough, therefore, to be your soldiers while you are at peace, but when war is declared they make off and disappear. I ought to have little difficulty in getting this believed, for the present ruin of Italy is due to no other cause than her having for many years trusted to mercenaries, who though heretofore they may have helped the fortunes of some one man, and made a show of strength when matched with one another, have always revealed themselves in their true colors so soon as foreign enemies appeared. Hence it was that Charles of France was suffered to conquer Italy with chalk; and he who said our sins were the cause, said truly, though it was not the sins he meant, but those which I have noticed. And as these were the sins of Princes, they it is who have paid the penalty.

But I desire to demonstrate still more clearly the untoward character of these forces. Captains of mercenaries are either able men or they are not. If they are, you cannot trust them, since they will always seek their own aggrandizement, either by overthrowing you who are their master, or by the overthrow of others contrary to your desire. On the other hand, if your captain be not an able man the chances are you will be ruined. And if it be said that whoever has arms in his hands will act in the same way whether he be a mercenary or no, I answer that when arms have to be employed by a Prince or a Republic, the Prince ought to go in person to take command as captain, the Republic should send one of her citizens, and if he proves incapable should change him, but if he prove capable should by the force of the laws confine him within proper bounds. And we see from experience that both Princes and Republics when they depend on their own arms have the greatest success, whereas from employing mercenaries nothing but loss results. Moreover, a Republic trusting to her own forces, is with greater difficulty than one which relies on foreign arms brought to yield obedience to a single citizen. Rome and Sparta remained for ages armed and free. The Swiss are at once the best armed and the freest people in the world. Of mercenary arms in ancient times we have an example in the Carthaginians, who at the close of their first war with Rome, were well-nigh ruined by their hired troops, although these were commanded by Carthaginian citizens. So too, when, on the death of Epaminondas, the Thebans made Philip of Macedon captain of their army, after gaining a victory for them, he deprived them of their liberty. The Milanese, in like manner, when Duke Filippo died, took Francesco Sforza into their pay to conduct the war against the Venetians. But he, after defeating the enemy at Caravaggio, combined with them to overthrow the Milanese, his masters. His father too while in the pay of Giovanna, Queen of

Naples, suddenly left her without troops, obliging her, in order to save her kingdom, to throw herself into the arms of the King of Aragon.

And if it be said that in times past the Venetians and the Florentines have extended their dominions by means of these arms, and that their captains have served them faithfully, without seeking to make themselves their masters, I answer that in this respect the Florentines have been fortunate, because among those valiant captains who might have given them cause for fear, some have not been victorious, some have had rivals, and some have turned their ambition in other directions.

Among those not victorious, was Giovanni Acuto, whose fidelity, since he was unsuccessful, was not put to the proof: but any one may see that had he been victorious, the Florentines must have been entirely in his hands. The Sforzas, again, had constant rivals in the Bracceschi, so that the one was a check upon the other; moreover, the ambition of Francesco was directed against Milan, while that of Braccio was directed against the Church and the kingdom of Naples. Let us turn, however, to what took place lately. The Florentines chose for their captain Paolo Vitelli, a most prudent commander, who had raised himself from privacy to the highest renown in arms. Had he been successful in reducing Pisa, none can deny that the Florentines would have been completely in his power, for they would have been ruined had he gone over to their enemies, while if they retained him they must have submitted to his will.

Again, as to the Venetians, if we consider the growth of their power, it will be seen that they conducted their affairs with glory and safety so long as their subjects of all ranks, gentle and simple alike, valiantly bore arms in their wars; as they did before they directed their enterprises landwards. But when they took to making war by land, they forsook those methods in which they excelled and were content to follow the customs of Italy.

At first, indeed, in extending their possessions on the mainland, having as yet but little territory and being held in high repute, they had not much to fear from their captains; but when their territories increased, which they did under Carmagnola, they were taught their mistake. For as they had found him a most valiant and skillful leader when, under his command, they defeated the Duke of Milan, and, on the other hand, saw him slack in carrying on the war, they made up their minds that no further victories were to be had under him; and because, through fear of losing what they had gained, they could not discharge him, to secure themselves against him they were forced to put him to death. After him they have had for captains, Bartolommeo of Bergamo, Roberto of San Severino, the Count of Pitigliano, and the like, under whom their danger has not been from victories, but from defeats; as, for instance, at Vaila, where they lost in a single day what it had taken the efforts of eight hundred years to acquire. For the gains resulting from mercenary arms are slow, and late, and inconsiderable, but the losses sudden and astounding.

And since these examples have led me back to Italy, which for many years past has been defended by mercenary arms, I desire to go somewhat deeper into the matter, in order that the causes which led to the adoption of these arms being seen, they may the more readily be corrected. You are to understand, then, that when in these later times the Imperial control began to be rejected by Italy, and the temporal power of the Pope to be more thought of, Italy suddenly split up into a number of separate States. For many of the larger cities took up arms against their nobles, who, with the favor of the Emperor, had before kept them in subjection, and were supported by the Church with a view to add to her temporal authority: while in many others of these cities, private citizens became rulers. Hence Italy, having passed almost entirely into the hands of the Church and of certain Republics, the former made up of priests, the latter of citizens unfamiliar with arms, began to take foreigners into her pay.

The first who gave reputation to this service was Alberigo of Conio in Romagna, from whose school of warlike training descended, among others, Braccio and Sforza, who in their time were the arbiters of Italy; after whom came all those others who down to the present hour have held similar commands, and to whose merits we owe it that our country has been overrun by Charles, plundered by Louis, wasted by Ferdinand, and insulted by the Swiss.

The first object of these mercenaries was to bring foot soldiers into disrepute, in order to enhance the merit of their own followers; and this they did, because lacking territory of their own and depending on their profession for their support, a few foot soldiers gave them no importance, while for a large number they were unable to provide. For these reasons they had recourse to horsemen, a less retinue of whom was thought to confer distinction, and could be more easily maintained. And the matter went to such a length, that in an army of twenty thousand men, not two thousand foot soldiers were to be found. Moreover, they spared no endeavor to relieve themselves and their men from fatigue and danger, not killing one another in battle, but making prisoners who were afterwards released without ransom. They would attack no town by night; those in towns would make no sortie by night against a besieging army. Their camps were without rampart or trench. They had no winter campaigns. All which arrangements were sanctioned by their military rules, contrived by them, as I have said already, to escape fatigue and danger; but the result of which has been to bring Italy into servitude and contempt.

Machiavelli's comments on soldiers of fortune are not consistent with the modern armed forces of the United States and what has come to be known as the economic draft[53] and the privatization of the military and veteran's benefits.[54] Modern soldiers fight for many reasons, only one of which is patriotism, but Machiavelli— who never fought a single battle—fails to recognize the influence of camaraderie of brothers and sisters in arms fighting merely out of

---

[53] Roberts, Maryam. "Economic Downturn Will Push More into the Military." *The Progressive*, 24 March 2009.

[54] Demirjian, Karoun "McCain and Veterans Aren't Always on the Same Page." *Washington Post*, 5 August 2016.

survival.[55] It is common knowledge that a strong offense, especially at night, precludes the need for defense. Clinton[56] and Trump[57] both, unfortunately, support privatization of the military. Stein[58] squarely opposes privatization of education and military, Johnson advocates for a stronger Congressional role in matters of war,[59] and Sanders has been a staunch critic of the Pentagon.[60]

---

[55] Sun Tzu. BrainyQuote.com, Xplore Inc, 2016.

[56] Scott, Timothy. "War and Wall Street: Clinton's Bleak Record." *Truthout*, 1 August 2016.

[57] Pollack, Norman "America and the Trump Conundrum." *Counter Punch*, 2 August 2016.

[58] Goodman, H.A. "Dr. Cornel West is Right, Jill Stein Should be America's First Female President." *Huffington Post*, 15 July 2016.

[59] Bush, Evan. "Thinking of Voting for Jill Stein or Gary Johnson? Here are their Policy Positions." *Seattle Times*, 1 August 2016.

[60] Hartung, William. "How Not to Audit the Pentagon." *Los Angeles Times*, 10 April 2016.

XIII. Of Auxiliary, Mixed, and National Arms

THE SECOND sort of unprofitable arms are auxiliaries, by whom I mean, troops brought to help and protect you by a potentate whom you summon to your aid; as when in recent times, Pope Julius II observing the pitiful behavior of his mercenaries at the enterprise of Ferrara, betook himself to auxiliaries, and arranged with Ferdinand of Spain to be supplied with horse and foot soldiers. Auxiliaries may be excellent and useful soldiers for themselves, but are always hurtful to him who calls them in; for if they are defeated, he is undone, if victorious, he becomes their prisoner. Ancient histories abound with instances of this, but I shall not pass from the example of Pope Julius, which is still fresh in men's minds. It was the height of rashness for him, in his eagerness to gain Ferrara, to throw himself without reserve into the arms of a stranger. Nevertheless, his good fortune came to his rescue, and he had not to reap the fruits of his ill-considered conduct. For after his auxiliaries were defeated at Ravenna, the Swiss suddenly descended and, to their own surprise and that of everyone else, swept the victors out of the country, so that, he neither remained a prisoner with his enemies, they being put to flight, nor with his auxiliaries, because victory was won by other arms than theirs. The Florentines, being wholly without soldiers of their own, brought ten thousand French men-at-arms to the siege of Pisa, thereby incurring greater peril than at any previous time of trouble. To protect himself from his neighbors, the Emperor of Constantinople summoned ten thousand Turkish soldiers into Greece, who, when the war was over, refused to leave, and this was the beginning of the servitude of Greece to the Infidel.

Let him, therefore, who would deprive himself of every chance of success, have recourse to auxiliaries, these being far more dangerous than mercenary arms, bringing ruin with them ready made. For they are united, and wholly under the control of their own officers; whereas, before mercenaries, even after gaining a victory, can do you hurt, longer time and better opportunities are needed; because, as they are made up of separate companies, raised and paid by you, he whom you place in command cannot at once acquire such authority over them as will be injurious to you. In short, with mercenaries your greatest danger is from their inertness and cowardice, with auxiliaries from their valor. Wise Princes, therefore, have always eschewed these arms, and trusted rather to their own, and have preferred defeat with the latter to victory with the former, counting that as no true victory which is gained by foreign aid.

I shall never hesitate to cite the example of Cesare Borgia and his actions. He entered Romagna with a force of auxiliaries, all of them French men-at-arms, with whom he took Imola and Forli. But it appearing to him afterwards that these troops were not to be trusted, he had recourse to mercenaries from whom he thought there would be less danger, and took the Orsini and Vitelli into his pay. But finding these likewise while under his command to be fickle, false, and treacherous, he got rid of them, and fell back on troops of his own raising. And we may readily discern the difference between these various kinds of arms, by observing the different degrees of reputation in which the Duke stood while he depended upon the French alone, when he took the Orsini and Vitelli into his pay, and when he fell back on his own troops and his own resources; for we find his reputation always increasing, and that he was never so well thought of as when everyone perceived him to be sole master of his own forces. I am unwilling to leave these examples, drawn from what has taken place in Italy and in recent times; and yet I must not omit to notice the case of Hiero of Syracuse, who is one of those whom I have already named. He, as I have before related, being made captain of their armies by the Syracusans, saw at once that a force of mercenary soldiers, supplied by men resembling our Italian condottieri, was not serviceable; and as he would not retain and could not disband them, he caused them all to be cut to pieces, and afterwards made war with native soldiers only, without other aid.

And here I would call to mind a passage in the Old Testament as bearing on this point. When David offered himself to Saul to go forth and fight Goliath the Philistine champion, Saul to encourage him armed him with his own armor, which David, so soon as he had put

*it on, rejected, saying that with these untried arms he could not
prevail, and that he chose rather to meet his enemy with only his
sling and his sword. In a word, the armor of others is too wide, or
too strait for us; it falls off us, or it weighs us down.*

*Charles VII, the father of Louis XI, who by his good fortune and
valor freed France from the English, saw this necessity of
strengthening himself with a national army, and drew up ordinances
regulating the service both of men-at-arms and of foot soldiers
throughout his kingdom. But afterwards his son, King Louis, did
away with the national infantry, and began to hire Swiss
mercenaries. Which blunder having been followed by subsequent
Princes, has been the cause, as the result shows, of the dangers into
which the kingdom of France has fallen; for, by enhancing the
reputation of the Swiss, the whole of the national troops of France
have been deteriorated. For from their infantry being done away
with, their men-at-arms are made wholly dependent on foreign
assistance, and being accustomed to co-operate with the Swiss, have
grown to think they can do nothing without them. Hence the French
are no match for the Swiss, and without them cannot succeed
against others.*

*The armies of France, then, are mixed, being partly national and
partly mercenary. Armies thus composed are far superior to mere
mercenaries or mere auxiliaries, but far inferior to forces purely
national. And this example is in itself conclusive, for the realm of
France would be invincible if the military ordinances of Charles VII
had been retained and extended. But from want of foresight men
make changes which relishing well at first do not betray their hidden
venom, as I have already observed respecting hectic fever.
Nevertheless, the ruler is not truly wise who cannot discern evils
before they develop themselves, and this is a faculty given to few.*

*If we look for the causes which first led to the overthrow of the
Roman Empire, they will be found to have had their source in the
employment of Gothic mercenaries, for from that hour the strength
of the Romans began to wane and all the virtue which went from*

them passed to the Goths. And, to be brief, I say that without national arms no Princedom is safe, but on the contrary is wholly dependent on Fortune, being without the strength that could defend it in adversity. And it has always been the deliberate opinion of the wise, that nothing is so infirm and fleeting as a reputation for power not founded upon a national army, by which I mean one composed of subjects, citizens, and dependents, all others being mercenary or auxiliary.

The methods to be followed for organizing a national army may readily be ascertained, if the rules above laid down by me, and by which I abide, be well considered, and attention be given to the manner in which Philip, father of Alexander the Great, and many other Princes and Republics have armed and disposed their forces.

Machiavelli shines through this chapter as uncooperative, nationalist, and racist as ever, especially toward the French. Trump echoes many of these sentiments with his disdain for anyone abroad or at home who does not look, act, and think like Trump.[61] Trump has even gone as far as to hint that some of his more zealous and violent followers pursue Second Amendment—assassination—options against Clinton simply because she does not share Trump's espoused views on gun ownership. Yet Clinton's foreign policy efforts to topple Gaddafi as a favor to Wall Street friends go well beyond the "treacherous" French that Machiavelli derides.[62] On the other hand, each of Sanders' four foreign policy promises squarely contradict Machiavelli in a much saner vision of world affairs:

1. Move away from a policy of unilateral military action, and toward a policy of emphasizing diplomacy, and ensuring the decision to go to war is a last resort.

---

[61] Lowe, Josh. "Trump Hits Out at Pope Over Mexico Visit." *Newsweek*, 12 February 2016.
[62] Hoff, Brad. "Hillary Emails Reveal True Motive for Libya Intervention." *Foreign Policy Journal*, 6 January 2016.

2. Ensure that any military action we do engage in has clear goals, is limited in scope, and whenever possible provides support to our allies in the region.
3. Close Guantanamo Bay, rein in the National Security Agency, abolish the use of torture, and remember what truly makes America exceptional: our values.
4. Expand our global influence by promoting fair trade, addressing global climate change, providing humanitarian relief and economic assistance, defending the rule of law, and promoting human rights.[63]

Johnson's vow to halve military spending[64] would drastically reduce world tensions and general warfare, while Stein's consistent pursuit of peace[65] would entirely undermine any need for Machiavelli's recommended machinations.

---

[63] https://berniesanders.com/issues/war-and-peace/
[64] "Gary Johnson Grabs GOP Third Rail: Cutting Military Spending." *Western Journalism*, 8 September 2011.
[65] Scott, Leslie. "The Story of Jill Stein: Putting Peace and Planet before Profits." *Counterpunch*, 4 May 2016.

XIV. Of the Duty of a Prince in Respect of Military Affairs

A PRINCE, therefore, should have no care or thought but for war, and for the regulations and training it requires, and should apply himself exclusively to this as his peculiar province; for war is the sole art looked for in one who rules, and is of such efficacy that it not merely maintains those who are born Princes, but often enables men to rise to that eminence from a private station; while, on the other hand, we often see that when Princes devote themselves rather to pleasure than to arms, they lose their dominions. And as neglect of this art is the prime cause of such calamities, so to be a proficient in it is the surest way to acquire power. Francesco Sforza, from his renown in arms, rose from privacy to be Duke of Milan, while his descendants, seeking to avoid the hardships and fatigues of military life, from being Princes fell back into privacy. For among other causes of misfortune which not being armed invites derision, and this is one of those reproaches against which, as shall presently be explained, a Prince ought most carefully to guard.

Between an armed and an unarmed man no proportion holds, and it is contrary to reason to expect that the armed man should voluntarily submit to him who is unarmed, or that the unarmed man should stand secure among armed retainers. For with contempt on one side, and distrust on the other, it is impossible that men should work well together. Wherefore, as has already been said, a Prince who is ignorant of military affairs, besides other disadvantages, can neither be respected by his soldiers, nor can he trust them. A Prince, therefore, ought never to allow his attention to be diverted from warlike pursuits, and should occupy himself with them even more in peace than in war. This he can do in two ways, by practice or by study.

As to the practice, he ought, besides keeping his soldiers well trained and disciplined, to be constantly engaged in the chase, that he may inure his body to hardships and fatigue, and gain at the same time a knowledge of places, by observing how the mountains slope, the valleys open, and the plains spread; acquainting himself with the characters of rivers and marshes, and giving the greatest attention to this subject. Such knowledge is useful to him in two ways; for first, he learns thereby to know his own country, and to understand better how it may be defended; and next, from his familiar acquaintance with its localities, he readily comprehends the character of other districts when obliged to observe them for the first time. For the hills, valleys, plains, rivers, and marshes of Tuscany, for example, have a certain resemblance to those elsewhere; so that from a knowledge of the natural features of that province, similar knowledge in respect of other provinces may readily be gained. The Prince who is wanting in this kind of knowledge, is wanting in the first qualification of a good captain for by it he is taught how to surprise an enemy, how to choose an encampment, how to lead his army on a march, how to array it for battle, and how to post it to the best advantage for a siege.

Among the commendations which Philopoemon, Prince of the Achaians, has received from historians is this—that in times of peace he was always thinking of methods of warfare, so that when walking in the country with his friends he would often stop and talk with them on the subject. 'If the enemy,' he would say, 'were posted on that hill, and we found ourselves here with our army, which of us would have the better position? How could we most safely and in the best order advance to meet them? If we had to retreat, what direction should we take? If they retired, how should we pursue?' In this way he put to his friends, as he went along, all the contingencies that can befall an army. He listened to their opinions, stated his own, and supported them with reasons; and from his being constantly occupied with such meditations, it resulted, that when in actual command no complication could ever present itself with which he was not prepared to deal. As to the mental training of which we have spoken, a Prince should read histories, and in these should note the actions of great men, observe how they conducted themselves in their wars, and examine the causes of their victories and defeats, so as to avoid the latter and imitate them in the former. And above all, he should, as many great men of past ages have done, assume for his models those persons who before his time have been renowned and celebrated, whose deeds and achievements he should constantly keep in mind, as it is related that Alexander the Great sought to resemble Achilles, Cæsar Alexander, and Scipio Cyrus. And anyone who reads the life of this last-named hero, written by Xenophon, recognizes afterwards in the life of Scipio, how much this imitation was the source of his glory, and how nearly in his chastity, affability, kindliness, and generosity, he conformed to the character of Cyrus as Xenophon describes it.

A wise Prince, therefore, should pursue such methods as these, never resting idle in times of peace, but strenuously seeking to turn them to account, so that he may derive strength from them in the hour of danger, and find himself ready should Fortune turn against him, to resist her blows.

Machiavelli is at his most wicked here, urging perpetual war. He even counsels preparing for war during times of peace. Clinton, as secretary of state, would seem to agree, especially with her meddling in Honduras and aggression in Libya.[66] As senator, she voted for the disastrous invasion of Iraq.[67] While Trump claims to be more isolationist, he is also clearly more volatile and likely to launch military strikes on whim.[68] Sanders, Johnson, and Stein each to varying degrees reject Machiavelli's advice "to be constantly engaged in the chase." The Declaration of Independence, though lists this notion of the standing army and quartering troops as one of the grievances against the King.[69]

---

[66] Shapiro, Jeffrey Scott and Kelly Riddell. "Secret Tapes Undermine Hillary Clinton on Libyan War." *Washington Times*, 28 January 2015.

[67] Landler, Mark. "How Hillary Became a Hawk." *New York Times*, 21 April 2016.

[68] Geiger, Kim. "Duckworth: Trump not Fit to be Commander in Chief." *Chicago Tribune*, 28 July 2016.

[69] Richman, Sheldon. "The Constitution and the Standing Army." *Counterpunch*, 29 February 2016.

XV. Of the Qualities in Respect of Which Men, and Most of all Princes, Are Praised or Blamed

IT now remains for us to consider what ought to be the conduct and bearing of a Prince in relation to his subjects and friends. And since I know that many have written on this subject, I fear it may be thought presumptuous in me to write of it also; the more so, because in my treatment of it, I depart from the views that others have taken.

But since it is my object to write what shall be useful to whosoever understands it, it seems to me better to follow the real truth of things than an imaginary view of them. For many Republics and Princedoms have been imagined that were never seen or known to exist in reality. And the manner in which we live, and that in which we ought to live, are things so wide asunder, that he who quits the one to betake himself to the other is more likely to destroy than to save himself; since anyone who would act up to a perfect standard of goodness in everything, must be ruined among so many who are not good. It is essential, therefore, for a Prince who desires to maintain his position, to have learned how to be other than good, and to use or not to use his goodness as necessity requires.

Laying aside, therefore, all fanciful notions concerning a Prince, and considering those only that are true, I say that all men when they are spoken of, and Princes more than others from their being set so high, are characterized by some one of those qualities which attach either praise or blame. Thus one is accounted liberal, another miserly (which word I use, rather than avaricious, to denote the man who is too sparing of what is his own, avarice being the disposition to take wrongfully what is another's); one is generous, another greedy; one cruel, another tender-hearted; one is faithless, another true to his word; one effeminate and cowardly, another high-spirited and courageous; one is courteous, another haughty; one impure, another chaste; one simple, another crafty; one firm, another facile; one grave, another frivolous; one devout, another unbelieving; and the like. Everyone, I know, will admit that it would be most laudable for a Prince to be endowed with all of the above qualities that are reckoned good; but since it is impossible for him to possess or constantly practice them all, the conditions of human nature not allowing it, he must be discreet enough to know how to avoid the infamy of those vices that would deprive him of his government, and, if possible, be on his guard also against those which might not deprive him of it; though if he cannot wholly restrain himself, he may with less scruple indulge in the latter. *He need never hesitate, however, to incur the reproach of those vices without which his authority can hardly be preserved; for if he well consider the whole matter, he will find that there may be a line of conduct having the appearance of virtue, to follow which would be his ruin, and that there may be another course having the appearance of vice, by following which his safety and well-being are secured.*

Machiavelli states here a version of his most famous recommendation to ruthlessness. Trump exemplifies the would be leader who never hesitates "to incur the reproach of those vices without which his authority can hardly be preserved," as Machiavelli puts it, and instead choses "to follow…another course having the appearance of vice, by which his safety and well-being are secured." So Trump is clearly no Superman for anyone to await.[70] Nor is Trump Godzilla, as Van Jones suggests.[71] He is, as some have opined, a dangerous clown,[72] as others have described him, a hateful demagogue,[73] but in the end, Trump will prove to be the monster to the Republican Party as Dr. Frankenstein. Trump is their creation, and he will soon become their demise, as Brookings Institution Senior Fellow Robert Kagan predicted in February of 2016.[74] Trump has derailed the GOP so dramatically that even

---

[70] Collins, Gail. "Waiting for Somebody." *New York Times*, 29 September, 2010.

[71] Jones, Van. "Trumpzilla." *Facebook*, 29 April 2016.

[72] McEnroe, Juno. "Donald Trump is a Racist and Dangerous Clown, Says John Halligan." *Irish Examiner*, 10 August 2016.

[73] Martin, Jonathan. "Meg Whitman, Calling Donald Trump a 'Demagogue,' Will Support Hillary Clinton for President." *New York Times*, 2 August 2016.

[74] Kagan, Robert. "Trump is GOP's Frankenstein: Now He's Strong Enough to Destroy the Party." *Washington Post*, 25 February 2016.

stalwart conservative commentator Glenn Beck has twice hosted Brad Thor, who advocated the assassination of Trump to save the party.[75]

---

[75] Chasmar, Jessica. "Glenn Beck suspended by SiriusXM after Brad Thor floats perceived assassination threat." *Washington Times*, 31 May 2016.

XVI. Of Liberality and Miserliness

BEGINNING, then, with the first of the qualities above noticed, I say that it may be a good thing to be reputed liberal, but, nevertheless, that liberality without the reputation of it is hurtful; because, though it be worthily and rightly used, still if it be not known, you escape not the reproach of its opposite vice. Hence, to have credit for liberality with the world at large, you must neglect no circumstance of sumptuous display; the result being, that a Prince of a liberal disposition will consume his whole substance in things of this sort, and, after all, be obliged, if he would maintain his reputation for liberality, to burden his subjects with extraordinary taxes, and to resort to confiscations and all the other shifts whereby money is raised. But in this way he becomes hateful to his subjects, and growing impoverished is held in little esteem by any. So that in the end, having by his liberality offended many and obliged few, he is worse off than when he began, and is exposed to all his original dangers. Recognizing this, and endeavoring to retrace his steps, he at once incurs the infamy of miserliness.

A Prince, therefore, since he cannot without injury to himself practice the virtue of liberality so that it may be known, will not, if he be wise, greatly concern himself though he be called miserly. Because in time he will come to be regarded as more and more liberal, when it is seen that through his parsimony his revenues are sufficient; that he is able to defend himself against any who make war on him; that he can engage in enterprises against others without burdening his subjects; and thus exercise liberality towards all from whom he does not take, whose number is infinite, while he is miserly in respect of those only to whom he does not give, whose number is few.

In our own days we have seen no Princes accomplish great results save those who have been accounted miserly. All others have been ruined. Pope Julius II, after availing himself of his reputation for liberality to arrive at the Papacy, made no effort to preserve that reputation when making war on the King of France, but carried on all his numerous campaigns without levying from his subjects a single extraordinary tax, providing for the increased expenditure out of his long-continued savings. Had the present King of Spain been accounted liberal, he never could have engaged or succeeded in so many enterprises. A Prince, therefore, if he is enabled thereby to forbear from plundering his subjects, to defend himself, to escape poverty and contempt, and the necessity of becoming rapacious, ought to care little though he incur the reproach of miserliness, for this is one of those vices which enable him to reign.

And should any object that Cæsar by his liberality rose to power, and that many others have been advanced to the highest dignities from their having been liberal and so reputed, I reply, "Either you are already a Prince or you seek to become one; in the former case liberality is hurtful, in the latter it is very necessary that you be thought liberal; Cæsar was one of those who sought the sovereignty of Rome; but if after obtaining it he had lived on without retrenching his expenditure, he must have ruined the Empire." And if it be further urged that many Princes reputed to have been most liberal have achieved great things with their armies, I answer that a Prince spends either what belongs to himself and his subjects, or what belongs to others; and that in the former case he ought to be sparing, but in the latter ought not to refrain from any kind of liberality. Because for a Prince who leads his armies in person and maintains them by plunder, pillage, and forced contributions, dealing as he does with the property of others this liberality is necessary, since otherwise he would not be followed by his soldiers. Of what does not belong to you or to your subjects you should, therefore, be a lavish giver, as were Cyrus, Cæsar, and Alexander; for to be liberal with the property of others does not take from your reputation, but adds to it. What injures you is to give away what is your own. And there is no quality so self-destructive as liberality; for while you practice it you lose the means whereby it can be practiced, and become poor and despised, or else, to avoid poverty, you become rapacious and hated. For liberality leads to one or other of these two results, against which, beyond all others, a Prince should guard.

Wherefore it is wiser to put up with the name of being miserly, which breeds ignominy, but without hate, than to be obliged, from the desire to be reckoned liberal, to incur the reproach of rapacity, which breeds hate as well as ignominy.

Machiavelli again inspires both Clinton and Trump in their celebrated, but likely insincere, philanthropy. Trump bragged so much about donating to veterans' groups that he encouraged journalists to test his veracity, only to find that Trump had collected millions for veterans but not dispersed the funds until caught and lambasted.[76] Clinton's family foundation has drawn even more scrutiny and criticism for venality.[77] Both Trump and Clinton also practice Machiavelli's advice that "a Prince who leads his armies in person and maintains them by plunder, pillage, and forced contributions,…liberality is necessary, since otherwise he would not be followed by his soldiers."

---

[76] Benen, Steve. "Trump's Veterans Controversy Goes from Bad to Worse." *MSNBC*, 1 June 2016.
[77] Sainato, Michael. "Clinton Foundation Corruption Should Be Next for the FBI." *Observer*, 13 July 2016.

XVII. Of Cruelty and Clemency, and Whether It Is Better to Be Loved or Feared

PASSING to the other qualities above referred to, I say that every Prince should desire to be accounted merciful and not cruel. Nevertheless, he should be on his guard against the abuse of this quality of mercy. Cesare Borgia was reputed cruel, yet his cruelty restored Romagna, united it, and brought it to order and obedience; so that if we look at things in their true light, it will be seen that he was in reality far more merciful than the people of Florence, who, to avoid the imputation of cruelty, suffered Pistoja to be torn to pieces by factions.

A Prince should therefore disregard the reproach of being thought cruel where it enables him to keep his subjects united and obedient. For he who quells disorder by a very few signal examples will in the end be more merciful than he who from too great leniency permits things to take their course and so to result in rapine and bloodshed; for these hurt the whole State, whereas the severities of the Prince injure individuals only.

And for a new Prince, of all others, it is impossible to escape a name for cruelty, since new States are full of dangers. Wherefore Virgil, by the mouth of Dido, excuses the harshness of her reign on the plea that it was new, saying, "A fate unkind, and newness in my reign Compel me thus to guard a wide domain."

Nevertheless, the new Prince should not be too ready of belief, nor too easily set in motion; nor should he himself be the first to raise alarms; but should so temper prudence with kindliness that too great confidence in others shall not throw him off his guard, nor groundless distrust render him insupportable.

And here comes in the question whether it is better to be loved rather than feared, or feared rather than loved. It might perhaps be answered that we should wish to be both; but since love and fear can hardly exist together, if we must choose between them, it is far safer to be feared than loved. For of men it may generally be affirmed, that they are thankless, fickle, false, studious to avoid danger, greedy of gain, devoted to you while you are able to confer benefits upon them, and ready, as I said before, while danger is distant, to shed their blood, and sacrifice their property, their lives, and their children for you; but in the hour of need they turn against you. The Prince, therefore, who without otherwise securing himself builds wholly on their professions is undone. For the friendships which we buy with a price, and do not gain by greatness and nobility of character, though they be fairly earned are not made good, but fail us when we have occasion to use them.

Moreover, men are less careful how they offend him who makes himself loved than him who makes himself feared. For love is held by the tie of obligation, which, because men are a sorry breed, is broken on every whisper of private interest; but fear is bound by the apprehension of punishment which never relaxes its grasp.

Nevertheless, a Prince should inspire fear in such a fashion that if he does not win love he may escape hate. For a man may very well be feared and yet not hated, and this will be the case so long as he does not meddle with the property or with the women of his citizens and subjects. And if constrained to put any to death, he should do so only when there is manifest cause or reasonable justification. But, above all, he must abstain from the property of others. For men will sooner forget the death of their father than the loss of their patrimony. Moreover, pretexts for confiscation are never to seek, and he who has once begun to live by rapine always finds reasons for taking what is not his; whereas reasons for shedding blood are fewer, and sooner exhausted.

But when a Prince is with his army, and has many soldiers under his command, he must needs disregard the reproach of cruelty, for without such a reputation in its Captain, no army can be held together or kept under any kind of control. Among other things remarkable in Hannibal this has been noted, that having a very great army, made up of men of many different nations and brought to fight in a foreign country, no dissension ever arose among the soldiers themselves, nor any mutiny against their leader, either in his good or in his evil fortunes. This we can only ascribe to the transcendent cruelty, which, joined with numberless great qualities, rendered him at once venerable and terrible in the eyes of his soldiers; for without this reputation for cruelty these other virtues would not have produced the like results.

Unreflecting writers, indeed, while they praise his achievements, have condemned the chief cause of them; but that his other merits would not by themselves have been so efficacious we may see from the case of Scipio, one of the greatest Captains, not of his own time only but of all times of which we have record, whose armies rose against him in Spain from no other cause than his too great leniency in allowing them a freedom inconsistent with military strictness. With which weakness Fabius Maximus taxed him in the Senate House, calling him the corrupter of the Roman soldiery. Again, when the Locrians were shamefully outraged by one of his lieutenants, he neither avenged them, nor punished the insolence of his officer; and this from the natural easiness of his disposition. So that it was said in the Senate by one who sought to excuse him, that there were many who knew better how to refrain from doing wrong themselves than how to correct the wrong-doing of others. This temper, however, must in time have marred the name and fame even of Scipio, had he continued in it, and retained his command. But living as he did under the control of the Senate, this hurtful quality was not merely disguised, but came to be regarded as a glory.

Returning to the question of being loved or feared, I sum up by saying, that since his being loved depends upon his subjects, while his being feared depends upon himself, a wise Prince should build on what is his own, and not on what rests with others. Only, as I have said, he must do his utmost to escape hatred.

Macchiavelli finally here in chapter 17 associates "cruelty" with "order" that injures "individuals only." Trump expressly agrees in his praising strongman Saddam Hussein precisely for "efficiency" in killing.[78] Clinton, too, has actively supported such vicious brutes as Mubarak in Egypt and the royal family in Saudi Arabia.[79] Sanders criticized Clinton's support in response to Clinton repudiating Sanders' favorable remarks toward the Nicaraguan Sandinistas, who overthrew brutal dictator Somoza.[80] Johnson rejects both drone strikes and boots on the ground as counterproductive,[81] and Stein call for an end to the so-called War on Drugs as cruelly racist.[82]

---

[78] Diamond, Jeremy. "Trump Praises Saddam Hussein's Efficient Killing of 'Terrorists,' Calls Today's Iraq 'Harvard for Terrorism.' " *CNN*, 6 July 2016.

[79] "Glenn Greenwald: Hillary Clinton Has Embraced Some of the Most Brutal Dictators in the World." *Democracy Now*, 24 March 2016

[80] Seitz-Wald, Alex. "The 25 Best Things We Learned from Bernie Sanders' Book." *MSNBC*, 28 May 2015.

[81] Geraghty, Jim. "Can Gary Johnson Gain Ground in a Time of Terror Attacks?" *National Review*, 20 June 2016.

[82] "Jill Stein on Drugs." *On the Issues*.

XVIII. How Princes Should Keep Faith

EVERYONE understands how praiseworthy it is in a Prince to keep faith, and to live uprightly and not craftily. Nevertheless, we see from what has taken place in our own days that Princes who have set little store by their word, but have known how to overreach men by their cunning, have accomplished great things, and in the end got the better of those who trusted to honest dealing.

Be it known, then, that there are two ways of contending, one in accordance with the laws, the other by force; the first of which is proper to men, the second to beasts. But since the first method is often ineffectual, it becomes necessary to resort to the second. A Prince should, therefore, understand how to use well both the man and the beast. And this lesson has been covertly taught by the ancient writers, who relate how Achilles and many others of these old Princes were given over to be brought up and trained by Chiron the Centaur; since the only meaning of their having for instructor one who was half man and half beast is, that it is necessary for a Prince to know how to use both natures, and that the one without the other has no stability.

But since a Prince should know how to use the beast's nature wisely, he ought of beasts to choose both the lion and the fox; for the lion cannot guard himself from the toils, nor the fox from wolves. He must therefore be a fox to discern toils, and a lion to drive off wolves.

To rely wholly on the lion is unwise; and for this reason a prudent Prince neither can nor ought to keep his word when to keep it is hurtful to him and the causes which led him to pledge it are removed. If all men were good, this would not be good advice, but since they are dishonest and do not keep faith with you, you in return, need not keep faith with them; and no prince was ever at a loss for plausible reasons to cloak a breach of faith. Of this numberless recent instances could be given, and it might be shown how many solemn treaties and engagements have been rendered inoperative and idle through want of faith in Princes, and that he who was best known to play the fox has had the best success. It is necessary, indeed, to put a good color on this nature, and to be skillful in simulating and dissembling. But men are so simple, and governed so absolutely by their present needs, that he who wishes to deceive will never fail in finding willing dupes. One recent example I will not omit. Pope Alexander VI had no care or thought but how to deceive, and always found material to work on. No man ever had a more effective manner of asseverating, or made promises with more solemn protestations, or observed them less. And yet, because he understood this side of human nature, his frauds always succeeded.

It is not essential, then, that a Prince should have all the good qualities which I have enumerated above, but it is most essential that he should seem to have them; I will even venture to affirm that if he has and invariably practices them all, they are hurtful, whereas the appearance of having them is useful. Thus, it is well to seem merciful, faithful, humane, religious, and upright, and also to be so; but the mind should remain so balanced that were it needful not to be so, you should be able and know how to change to the contrary.

And you are to understand that a Prince, and most of all a new Prince, cannot observe all those rules of conduct in respect whereof men are accounted good, being often forced, in order to preserve his Princedom, to act in opposition to good faith, charity, humanity, and religion. He must therefore keep his mind ready to shift as the winds and tides of Fortune turn, and, as I have already said, he ought not to quit good courses if he can help it, but should know how to follow evil courses if he must.

A Prince should therefore be very careful that nothing ever escapes his lips which is not replete with the five qualities above named, so that to see and hear him, one would think him the embodiment of mercy, good faith, integrity, humanity, and religion. And there is no virtue which it is more necessary for him to seem to possess than this last; because men in general judge rather by the eye than by the hand, for every one can see but few can touch. Everyone sees what you seem, but few know what you are, and these few dare not oppose themselves to the opinion of the many who have the majesty of the State to back them up.

Moreover, in the actions of all men, and most of all of Princes, where there is no tribunal to which we can appeal, we look to results. Wherefore, if a Prince succeeds in establishing and maintaining his authority, the means will always be judged honorable and be approved by everyone. For the vulgar are always taken by appearances and by results, and the world is made up of the vulgar, the few only finding room when the many have no longer ground to stand on.

A certain Prince of our own days, whose name it is as well not to mention, is always preaching peace and good faith, although the mortal enemy of both; and both, had he practiced them as he preaches them, would, oftener than once, have lost him his kingdom and authority.

Machiavelli ends this chapter by mocking a contemporary first for hypocrisy but ultimately for considering peace and good faith as weakness and sure paths to failure. Clinton, too, often cloaks her hawkish foreign policy adventures in the guise of humanitarian causes while attempting to stifle any who expose her.[83] Trump's primary campaign has banked on the taking "the vulgar" by "appearances," hoping that the American electorate is "made up [primarily] of the vulgar," but this strategy seems to be undermining his flagging general election campaign poll numbers, prompting him to complain of chicanery.[84] Sanders' campaign thoroughly disproved Machiavelli's argument that it is more important to "seem to possess" a quality than authentically possess it, as Obama himself

---

[83] Parry, Robert. "Hillary Clinton's Hypocrisy on Dissent." *Consortium News*, 18 February 2016.
[84] Gonyea, Don. "As Trump Poll Numbers Slip, He Warns of a Rigged Election." *NPR*, 6 August 2016.

noticed in Sanders.[85] Johnson's campaign appeals to much more human and intellectual aspirations that beastly deceptions or frauds preying on the "dupes" that Machiavelli derides.[86] Stein's popularity stems exactly from her demonstrated rejection of Machiavelli's advice that a leader must be able to follow "evil" courses if necessary.[87]

[85] Kasperowicz, Pete. "Obama gives Sanders the edge over Clinton on 'authenticity.' " *Washington Examiner*, 25 January 2016.

[86] "Gary Johnson is an Honest but Defective Candidate." *Washington Post*." 7 July 2016.

[87] Reston, Laura. "Is Jill Stein the Next Ralph Nader?" *New Republic* 2 June 2016.

XIX. That a Prince Should Seek to Escape Contempt and Hatred

HAVING now spoken of the chief of the qualities above referred to, the rest I shall dispose of briefly with these general remarks, that a Prince, as has already in part been said, should consider how he may avoid such courses as would make him hated or despised; and that whenever he succeeds in keeping clear of these, he has performed his part, and runs no risk though he incur other infamies.

A Prince, as I have said before, sooner becomes hated by being rapacious and by interfering with the property and with the women of his subjects than in any other way. From these, therefore, he should abstain. For so long as neither their property nor their honor is touched, the mass of mankind live contentedly, and the Prince has only to cope with the ambition of a few, which can in many ways and easily be kept within bounds.

A Prince is despised when he is seen to be fickle, frivolous, effeminate, pusillanimous, or irresolute, against which defects he ought therefore most carefully to guard, striving so to bear himself that greatness, courage, wisdom, and strength may appear in all his actions. In his private dealings with his subjects his decisions should be irrevocable, and his reputation such that no one would dream of overreaching or cajoling him.

The Prince who inspires such an opinion of himself is greatly esteemed, and against one who is greatly esteemed conspiracy is difficult; nor, when he is known to be an excellent Prince and held in reverence by his subjects, will it be easy to attack him. For a Prince is exposed to two dangers, from within in respect of his subjects, from without in respect of foreign powers. Against the latter he will defend himself with good arms and good allies, and if he maintains good arms he will always have good allies; and when things are settled abroad, they will always be settled at home, unless disturbed by conspiracies; and even should there be hostility from without, if he has taken those measures, and has lived in the way I have recommended, and if he never abandons hope, he will withstand every attack; as I have said was done by Nabis the Spartan.

As regards his own subjects, when affairs are quiet abroad, he has to fear they may engage in secret plots; against which a Prince best secures himself when he escapes being hated or despised, and keeps on good terms with his people; and this, as I have already shown at length, it is essential he should do. Not to be hated or despised by the body of his subjects, is one of the surest safeguards that a Prince can have against conspiracy. For he who conspires always reckons on pleasing the people by putting the Prince to death; but when he sees that instead of pleasing he will offend them, he cannot summon courage to carry out his design. For the difficulties that attend conspirators are infinite, and we know from experience that while there have been many conspiracies, few of them have succeeded.

He who conspires cannot do so alone, nor can he assume as his companions any save those whom he believes to be discontented; but so soon as you impart your design to a discontented man, you supply him with the means of removing his discontent, since by betraying you he can procure for himself every advantage; so that seeing on the one hand certain gain, and on the other a doubtful and dangerous risk, he must either be a rare friend to you, or the mortal enemy of his Prince, if he keep your secret.

To put the matter shortly, I say that on the side of the conspirator there are distrust, jealousy, and dread of punishment to deter him, while on the side of the Prince there are the laws, the majesty of the throne, the protection of friends and of the government to defend him; to which if the general good-will of the people be added, it is hardly possible that any should be rash enough to conspire. For while in ordinary cases, the conspirator has ground for fear only before the execution of his villainy, in this case he has also cause to fear after the crime has been perpetrated, since he has the people for his enemy, and is thus cut off from every hope of shelter. Of this, endless instances might be given, but I shall content myself with one that happened within the recollection of our fathers. Messer Annibale Bentivoglio, Lord of Bologna and grandfather of the present Messer Annibale, was conspired against and murdered by the Canneschi, leaving behind none belonging to him save Messer Giovanni, then an infant in arms. Immediately upon the murder, the people rose and put all the Canneschi to death. This resulted from the general goodwill with which the House of the Bentivogli was then regarded in Bologna; which feeling was so strong, that when upon the death of Messer Annibale no one was left who could govern the State, there being reason to believe that a descendant of the family (who up to that time had been thought to be the son of a smith), was living in Florence, the citizens of Bologna came there for him, and entrusted him with the government of their city; which he retained until Messer Giovanni was old enough to govern.

To be brief, a Prince has little to fear from conspiracies when his subjects are well disposed towards him; but when they are hostile and hold him in detestation, he has then reason to fear everything and everyone. And well-ordered States and wise Princes have provided with extreme care that the nobility shall not be driven to desperation, and that the commons shall be kept satisfied and contented; for this is one of the most important matters that a Prince has to look to.

Among the well-ordered and governed Kingdoms of our day is that of France, wherein we find an infinite number of wise institutions, upon which depend the freedom and the security of the King, and of which the most important are the Parliament and its authority. For he who gave its constitution to this Realm, knowing the ambition and arrogance of the nobles, and judging it necessary to bridle and restrain them, and on the other hand knowing the hatred, originating in fear, entertained against them by the commons, and desiring that they should be safe, was unwilling that the responsibility for this should rest on the King; and to relieve him of the ill-will which he might incur with the nobles by favoring the commons, or with the commons by favoring the nobles, appointed a third party to be arbitrator, who without committing the King, might depress the nobles and uphold the commons. Nor could there be any better, wiser, or surer safeguard for the King and the Kingdom. And hence we may draw another notable lesson, namely, that Princes should devolve on others those matters that entail responsibility, and reserve to themselves those that relate to grace and favor. And again I say that a Prince should esteem the great, but must not make himself odious to the people.

To some it may perhaps appear, that if the lives and deaths of many of the Roman Emperors be considered, they offer examples opposed to the views expressed by me; since we find that some among them who had always lived good lives, and shown themselves possessed of great qualities, were nevertheless deposed and even put to death by their subjects who had conspired against them.

In answer to such objections, I shall examine the characters of several Emperors, and show that the causes of their downfall were in no way different from those which I have indicated. In doing this I shall submit for consideration such matters only as must strike everyone who reads the history of these times; and it will be enough for my purpose to take those Emperors who reigned from the time of Marcus the Philosopher to the time of Maximinus, who were, inclusively, Marcus, Commodus his son, Pertinax, Julianus, Severus, Caracalla his son, Macrinus, Heliogabalus, Alexander, and Maximinus. In the first place, then, we have to note that while in other Princedoms the Prince has only to contend with the ambition of the nobles and the insubordination of the people, the Roman Emperors had a further difficulty to encounter in the cruelty and rapacity of their soldiers, which were so distracting as to cause the ruin of many of these Princes. For it was hardly possible for them to satisfy both the soldiers and the people; the latter loving peace and therefore preferring sober Princes, while the former preferred a Prince of a warlike spirit, however harsh, haughty, or rapacious; being willing that he should exercise these qualities against the people, as the means of procuring for themselves double pay, and indulging their greed and cruelty.

Whence it followed that those Emperors who had not inherited or won for themselves such authority as enabled them to keep both people and soldiers in check, were always ruined. The most of them, and those especially who came to the Empire new and without experience, seeing the difficulty of dealing with these conflicting humors, set themselves to satisfy the soldiers, and made little account of offending the people. And for them this was a necessary course to take; for as Princes cannot escape being hated by some, they should, in the first place, endeavor not to be hated by a class; failing in which, they must do all they can to escape the hatred of that class which is the stronger. Wherefore those Emperors who, by reason of their newness, stood in need of extraordinary support, sided with the soldiery rather than with the people; a course which turned out advantageous or otherwise, according as the Prince knew, or did not know, how to maintain his authority over them.

From the causes indicated it resulted that Marcus, Pertinax, and Alexander, being Princes of a temperate disposition, lovers of justice, enemies of cruelty, gentle, and kindly, had all, save Marcus, an unhappy end. Marcus alone lived and died honored in the highest degree; and this because he had succeeded to the Empire by right of inheritance, and not through the favor either of the army or of the people; and also because, being endowed with many virtues which made him revered, he kept, while he lived, both factions within bounds, and was never either hated or despised.

But Pertinax was chosen Emperor against the will of the soldiery, who being accustomed to a licentious life under Commodus, could not tolerate the stricter discipline to which his successor sought to bring them back. And having thus made himself hated, and being at the same time despised by reason of his advanced age, he was ruined at the very outset of his reign.

And here it is to be noted that hatred is incurred as well on account of good actions as of bad; for which reason, as I have already said, a Prince who would maintain his authority is often compelled to be other than good. For when the class, be it the people, the soldiers, or the nobles, on whom you judge it necessary to rely for your support, is corrupt, you must needs adapt yourself to its humors, and satisfy these, in which case virtuous conduct will only prejudice you.

Let us now come to Alexander, who was so just a ruler that among the praises ascribed to him it is recorded, that, during the fourteen years he held the Empire, no man was ever put to death by him without trial. Nevertheless, being accounted effeminate, and thought to be governed by his mother, he fell into contempt, and the army conspiring against him, slew him.

When we turn to consider the characters of Commodus, Severus, and Caracalla, we find them all to have been cruelest and most rapacious Princes, who to satisfy the soldiery, scrupled not to inflict every kind of wrong upon the people. And all of them, except Severus, came to a bad end. But in Severus there was such strength of character, that, keeping the soldiers his friends, he was able, although he oppressed the people, to reign on prosperously to the last; because his great qualities made him so admirable in the eyes both of the people and the soldiers, that the former remained in a manner amazed and awestruck, while the latter were respectful and contented.

And because his actions, for one who was a new Prince, were thus remarkable, I will point out shortly how well he understood to play the part both of the lion and of the fox, each of which natures, as I have observed before, a Prince should know how to assume.

Knowing the indolent disposition of the Emperor Julianus, Severus persuaded the army which he commanded in Illyria that it was their duty to go to Rome to avenge the death of Pertinax, who had been slain by the Pretorian guards. Under this pretext, and without disclosing his design on the Empire, he put his army in march, and reached Italy before it was known that he had set out. On his arrival in Rome, the Senate, through fear, elected him Emperor and put Julianus to death. After taking this first step, two obstacles still remained to his becoming sole master of the Empire; one in Asia, where Niger who commanded the armies of the East had caused himself to be proclaimed Emperor; the other in the West, where Albinus, who also aspired to the Empire, was in command. And as Severus judged it dangerous to declare open war against both, he resolved to proceed against Niger by arms, and against Albinus by artifice. To the latter, accordingly, he wrote, that having been chosen Emperor by the Senate, he desired to share the dignity with him; that he therefore sent him the title of Caesar, and in accordance with a resolution of the Senate assumed him as his colleague. All which statements Albinus accepted as true. But so soon as Severus had defeated and slain Niger, and restored tranquility in the East, returning to Rome he complained in the Senate that Albinus, all unmindful of the favors he had received from him, had treacherously sought to destroy him; for which cause he was compelled to go and punish his ingratitude. Whereupon he set forth to seek Albinus in Gaul, where he at once deprived him of his dignities and his life.

Whoever, therefore, examines carefully the actions of this Emperor, will find in him all the fierceness of the lion and all the craft of the fox, and will note how he was feared and respected by the people, yet not hated by the army, and will not be surprised that though a new man, he was able to maintain his hold of so great an Empire. For the splendor of his reputation always shielded him from the odium which the people might otherwise have conceived against him by reason of his cruelty and rapacity.

Caracalla, his son, was likewise a man of great parts, endowed with qualities that made him admirable in the sight of the people, and endeared him to the army, being of a warlike spirit, most patient of fatigue, and contemning all luxury in food and every other effeminacy. Nevertheless, his ferocity and cruelty were so extravagant and unheard of (he having put to death a vast number of the inhabitants of Rome at different times, and the whole of those of Alexandria at a stroke), that he came to be detested by all the world, and so feared even by those whom he had about him, that at the last he was slain by a centurion in the midst of his army. And here let it be noted that deaths like this which are the result of a deliberate and fixed resolve, cannot be escaped by Princes, since anyone who disregards his own life can affect them. A Prince, however, needs the less to fear them as they are seldom attempted. The only precaution he can take is to avoid doing grave wrong to any of those who serve him, or whom he has near him as officers of his Court, a precaution which Caracalla neglected in putting to a shameful death the brother of this centurion, and in using daily threats against the man himself, whom he nevertheless retained as one of his bodyguard. This, as the event showed, was a rash and fatal course.

We come next to Commodus, who, as he took the Empire by hereditary right, ought to have held it with much ease. For being the son of Marcus, he had only to follow in his father's footsteps to content both the people and the army. But being of a cruel and brutal nature, to sate his rapacity at the expense of the people, he sought support from the army, and indulged it in every kind of excess. On the other hand, by an utter disregard of his dignity, in frequently descending into the arena to fight with gladiators, and by other base acts wholly unworthy of the Imperial station, he became contemptible in the eyes of the army; and being on the one hand hated, on the other despised, was at last conspired against and murdered.

The character of Maximinus remains to be touched upon. He was of a very warlike disposition, and on the death of Alexander, of whom we have already spoken, was chosen Emperor by the army who had been displeased with the effeminacy of that Prince. But this dignity he did not long enjoy, since two causes concurred to render him at once odious and contemptible; the one the baseness of his origin, he having at one time herded sheep in Thrace, a fact well known to all, and which led all to look on him with disdain; the other that on being proclaimed Emperor, delaying to repair to Rome and enter on possession of the Imperial throne, he incurred the reputation of excessive cruelty by reason of the many atrocities perpetrated by his prefects in Rome and other parts of the Empire. The result was that the whole world, stirred at once with scorn of his mean birth and with the hatred which the dread of his ferocity inspired, combined against him, Africa leading the way, the Senate and people of Rome and the whole of Italy following. In which conspiracy his own army joined. For they, being engaged in the siege of Aquileja and finding difficulty in reducing it, disgusted with his cruelty, and less afraid of him when they saw so many against him, put him to death.

I need say nothing of Heliogabalus, Macrinus, or Julianus, all of whom being utterly despicable, came to a speedy downfall, but shall conclude these remarks by observing, that the Princes of our own days are less troubled with the difficulty of having to make constant efforts to keep their soldiers in good humor. For though they must treat them with some indulgence, the need for doing so is soon over, since none of these Princes possesses a standing army which, like the armies of the Roman Empire, has strengthened with the growth of his government and the administration of his State. And if it was then necessary to satisfy the soldiers rather than the people, because the soldiers were more powerful than the people, now it is more necessary for all Princes, except the Turk and the Soldan, to satisfy the people rather than the soldiers, since the former are more powerful than the latter. I except the Turk because he has always about him some twelve thousand foot soldiers and fifteen thousand horses, on whom depend the security and strength of his kingdom, and with whom he must keep on good terms, all regard for the people being subordinate. The government of the Soldan is similar, so that he too being wholly in the hands of his soldiers, must keep well with them without regard to the people.

And here you are to note that the State of the Soldan, while it is unlike all other Princedoms, resembles the Christian Pontificate in this, that it can neither be classed as new, nor as hereditary. For the sons of a Soldan who dies do not succeed to the kingdom as his heirs, but he who is elected to the post by those who have authority to make such elections. And this being the ancient and established order of things, the Princedoms cannot be accounted new, since none of the difficulties that attend new Princedoms are found in it.

For although the Prince be new, the institutions of the State are old, and are so contrived that the elected Prince is accepted as though he were an hereditary Sovereign.

But returning to the matter in hand, I say that whoever reflects on the above reasoning will see that either hatred or contempt was the ruin of the Emperors whom I have named; and will also understand how it happened that some taking one way and some the opposite, one only by each of these roads came to a happy, and all the rest to an unhappy end. Because for Pertinax and Alexander, they being new Princes, it was useless and hurtful to try to imitate Marcus, who was an hereditary Prince; and similarly for Caracalla, Commodus, and Maximinus it was a fatal error to imitate Severus, since they lacked the qualities that would have enabled them to tread in his footsteps.

In short, a Prince new to the Princedom cannot imitate the actions of Marcus, nor is it necessary that he should imitate all those of Severus; but he should borrow from Severus those parts of his conduct which are needed to serve as a foundation for his government, and from Marcus those suited to maintain it, and render it glorious when once established.

Machiavelli creates here nothing short of an absolute dictator, whose "decisions should be irrevocable, and [whose] reputation such that no one would dream of overreaching or cajoling him." Machiavelli celebrates Emperor Severus not for his service to his people but for his skill at propaganda: "For the splendor of his reputation always shielded him from the odium which the people might otherwise have conceived against him by reason of his cruelty and rapacity." Trump's repeated calls to let Trump "fix it," is an invitation for voters to elect Trump as a dictator who reports his edicts to them at his discretion.[88] Clinton's "lion and fox" routine is perhaps more subtle than Trump's, but her celebration of the execution of Qaddafi would do Machiavelli proud.[89] Sanders, like Machiavelli's

---

[88] Appelbaum, Yoni. "'I Alone Can Fix it.'" *The Atlantic*, 21 July 2016.

description of Alexander, is so "effeminate" as to insist on due process and rule of law.[90] Johnson was so uninterested in war-mongering that he was unaware that Aleppo was the sight of much warfare in Syria.[91] In early September 2016, Stein showed her compassion and adherence to "virtuous conduct" by protesting with the Standing Rock Sioux opposing the oil pipeline project threatening their water supply.[92]

[89] Daly, Corbett. "Clinton on Qaddafi: 'We Came, We Saw, He Died.'" *CBS News*, 20 October 2011.
[90] Howe, Caleb. "Bernie Sanders: If You Think I'm a Radical, Just Listen to This Pope." *Truth Revolt*, 24 September 2015.
[91] Rappeport, Alan. "Gary Johnson's 'What Is Aleppo' Flub Amplifies Skepticism of Republicans." *New York Times*, 9 September 2016.
[92] Nichols, John. "There Is an Arrest Warrant Out for Jill Stein." *The Nation*, 9 September 2016.

XX. Whether Fortresses, and Certain Other Expedients to Which Princes Often Have Recourse, Are Profitable or Hurtful

TO govern more securely some Princes have disarmed their subjects, others have kept the towns subject to them divided by factions; some have fostered hostility against themselves, others have sought to gain over those who at the beginning of their reign were looked on with suspicion; some have built fortresses, others have dismantled and destroyed them; and though no definite judgment can be pronounced respecting any of these methods, without regard to the special circumstances of the State to which it is proposed to apply them, I shall nevertheless speak of them in as comprehensive a way as the nature of the subject will admit.

It has never chanced that any new Prince has disarmed his subjects. On the contrary, when he has found them unarmed he has always armed them. For the arms thus provided become yours, those whom you suspected grow faithful, while those who were faithful at the first, continue so, and from your subjects become your partisans. And though all your subjects cannot be armed, yet if those of them whom you arm be treated with marked favor, you can deal more securely with the rest. For the difference which those whom you supply with arms perceive in their treatment, will bind them to you, while the others will excuse you, recognizing that those who incur greater risk and responsibility merit greater rewards. But by disarming, you at once give offence, since you show your subjects that you distrust them, either as doubting their courage, or as doubting their fidelity, each of which imputations begets hatred against you.

Moreover, as you cannot maintain yourself without arms you must have recourse to mercenary troops. What these are I have already shown, but even if they were good, they could never avail to defend you, at once against powerful enemies abroad and against subjects whom you distrust. Wherefore, as I have said already, new Princes in new Princedoms have always provided for their being armed; and of instances of this History is full. But when a Prince acquires a new

State, which thus becomes joined on like a limb to his old possessions, he must disarm its inhabitants, except such of them as have taken part with him while he was acquiring it; and even these, as time and occasion serve, he should seek to render soft and effeminate; and he must so manage matters that all the arms of the new State shall be in the hands of his own soldiers who have served under him in his ancient dominions.

Our forefathers, even such among them as were esteemed wise, were wont to say that 'Pistoja was to be held by feuds, and Pisa by fortresses,' and on this principle used to promote dissensions in various subject towns with a view to retain them with less effort. At a time when Italy was in some measure in equilibrium, this may have been a prudent course to follow; but at the present day it seems impossible to recommend it as a general rule of policy. For I do not believe that divisions purposely caused can ever lead to good; on the contrary, when an enemy approaches, divided cities are lost at once, for the weaker faction will always side with the invader, and the other will not be able to stand alone.

The Venetians, influenced as I believe by the reasons above mentioned, fostered the factions of Guelf and Ghibelline in the cities subject to them; and though they did not suffer blood to be shed, fomented their feuds, in order that the citizens having their minds occupied with these disputes might not conspire against them. But this, as we know, did not turn out to their advantage, for after their defeat at Vaila, one of the two factions, suddenly taking courage, deprived them of the whole of their territory.

Moreover, methods like these argue weakness in a Prince, for under a strong government such divisions would never be permitted, since they are profitable only in time of peace as an expedient whereby subjects may be more easily managed; but when war breaks out their insufficiency is demonstrated.

Doubtless, Princes become great by vanquishing difficulties and opposition, and Fortune, on that account, when she desires to

*aggrandize a new Prince, who has more need than an hereditary
Prince to win reputation, causes enemies to spring up, and urges
them on to attack him, to the end that he may have opportunities to
overcome them, and make his ascent by the very ladder which they
have planted. For which reason, many are of the opinion that a wise
Prince, when he has the occasion, ought dexterously to promote
hostility to himself in certain quarters, in order that his greatness
may be enhanced by crushing it.*

*Princes, and new Princes especially, have found greater fidelity and
helpfulness in those whom, at the beginning of their reign, they have
held in suspicion, than in those who at the outset have enjoyed their
confidence; and Pandolfo Petrucci, Lord of Siena, governed his
State by the instrumentality of those whom he had at one time
distrusted, in preference to all others. But on this point it is
impossible to lay down any general rule, since the course to be
followed varies with the circumstances. This only I will say, that
those men who at the beginning of a reign have been hostile, if of a
sort requiring support to maintain them, may always be won over by
the Prince with much ease, and are the more bound to serve him
faithfully because they know that they have to efface by their
conduct the unfavorable impression he had formed of them; and in
this way a Prince always obtains better help from them, than from
those who serving him in too complete security neglect his affairs.
And since the subject suggests it, I must not fail to remind the Prince
who acquires a new State through the favor of its inhabitants, to
weigh well what were the causes which led those who favored him to
do so; and if it be seen that they have acted not from any natural
affection for him, but merely out of discontent with the former
government, that he will find the greatest difficulty in keeping them
his friends, since it will be impossible for him to content them.
Carefully considering the cause of this, with the aid of examples
taken from times ancient and modern, he will perceive that it is far
easier to secure the friendship of those who being satisfied with
things as they stood, were for that very reason his enemies, than of
those who sided with him and aided him in his usurpation only
because they were discontented.*

It has been customary for Princes, with a view to hold their dominions more securely, to build fortresses which might serve as a curb and restraint on such as have designs against them, and as a safe refuge against a first onset. I approve this custom, because it has been followed from the earliest times. Nevertheless, in our own days, Messer Niccolo Vitelli thought it prudent to dismantle two fortresses in Città di Castello in order to secure that town: and Guido Ubaldo, Duke of Urbino, on returning to his dominions, whence he had been driven by Cesare Borgia, razed to their foundations the fortresses throughout the Dukedom, judging that if these were removed, it would not again be so easily lost. A like course was followed by the Bentivogli on their return to Bologna.

Fortresses, therefore, are useful or no, according to circumstances, and if in one way they benefit, in another they injure you. We may state the case thus: The Prince who is more afraid of his subjects than of strangers ought to build fortresses, while he who is more afraid of strangers than of his subjects, should leave them alone. The citadel built by Francesco Sforza in Milan, has been, and will hereafter prove to be, more dangerous to the House of Sforza than any other disorder of that State. So that, on the whole, the best fortress you can have, is in not being hated by your subjects. If they hate you no fortress will save you; for when once the people take up arms, foreigners are never wanting to assist them.

Within our own time it does not appear that fortresses have been of service to any Prince, unless to the Countess of Forli after her husband Count Girolamo was murdered; for by this means she was able to escape the first onset of the insurgents, and awaiting succor from Milan, to recover her State; the circumstances of the times not allowing any foreigner to lend assistance to the people. But afterwards, when she was attacked by Cesare Borgia, and the people, out of hostility to her, took part with the invader, her fortresses were of little avail. So that, both on this and on the former occasion, it would have been safer for her to have had no fortresses, than to have had her subjects for enemies.

*All which considerations taken into account, I shall applaud him
who builds fortresses, and him who does not; but I shall blame him
who, trusting in them, reckons it a light thing to be held in hatred by
his people.*

Machiavelli is at his most cynical here, advising "that a wise Prince,
when he has the occasion, ought dexterously to promote hostility to
himself in certain quarters, in order that his greatness may be
enhanced by crushing it." Trump regularly slights reporters publicly
only to attack them more vehemently when they criticize his
rudeness.[93] Trump's supporters typically view Trump's oafish
bullying of others as strength.[94] But, playing on Trump's
manipulations, Clinton likely encouraged the Democratic
Convention organizers to present the Khan family to celebrate the
bravery of their United States Army veteran son while challenging
Trump by waving a pocket Constitution in the air to denounce
Trump as ignorant and of it and hostile towards its principles.
Trump responded, as expected, by attacking the Khans, but this time
Trump had gone too far, and Republican operatives urged Trump to
recant.[95] Sanders proposes building of coalition, not creating
factions, in response to the quagmire in Syria.[96]

---

[93] Donald Trump Resorts to Insulting Reporters During Heated Press
Conference." *The Week*, 31 May 2016.
[94] Kafer, Krista. "Why Trump's Supporters Like Him So Much." *The Federalist*, 1
February 2016.
[95] Bradner, Eric. "Did Trump Go Too Far?" *CNN*, 1 August 2016.
[96] Greenberg, Jon. "Clinton Says Sanders Proposed Iranian Troops in Syria."
Politifact, 5 February 2016.

XXI. How a Prince Should Bear Himself
So as to Acquire Reputation

NOTHING makes a Prince so well thought of as to undertake great enterprises and give striking proofs of his capacity. Among the Princes of our time Ferdinand of Aragon, the present King of Spain, may almost be accounted a new Prince, since from one of the weakest he has become, for fame and glory, the foremost King in Christendom. And if you consider his achievements you will find them all great and some extraordinary.

In the beginning of his reign he made war on Granada, which enterprise was the foundation of his power. At first he carried on the war leisurely, without fear of interruption, and kept the attention and thoughts of the Barons of Castile so completely occupied with it, that they had no time to think of changes at home. Meanwhile he insensibly acquired reputation among them and authority over them. With the money of the Church and of his subjects he was able to maintain his armies, and during the prolonged contest to lay the foundations of that military discipline which afterwards made him so famous. Moreover, to enable him to engage in still greater undertakings, always covering himself with the cloak of religion, he had recourse to what may be called pious cruelty, in driving out and clearing his Kingdom of the Moors; than which exploit none could be more wonderful or uncommon. Using the same pretext he made war on Africa, invaded Italy, and finally attacked France; and being thus constantly busied in planning and executing vast designs, he kept the minds of his subjects in suspense and admiration, and occupied with the results of his actions, which arose one out of another in such close succession as left neither time nor opportunity to oppose them.

Again, it greatly profits a Prince in conducting the internal government of his State, to follow striking methods, such as are recorded of Messer Bernabo of Milan, whenever the remarkable actions of any one in civil life, whether for good or for evil, afford him occasion; and to choose such ways of rewarding and punishing as cannot fail to be much spoken of. But above all, he should strive by all his actions to inspire a sense of his greatness and goodness.

A Prince is likewise esteemed who is a stanch friend and a thorough foe, that is to say, who without reserve openly declares for one against another, this being always a more advantageous course than to stand neutral. For supposing two of your powerful neighbors come to blows, it must either be that you have, or have not, reason to fear the one who comes off victorious. In either case it will always be well for you to declare yourself, and join in frankly with one side or other. For should you fail to do so you are certain, in the former of the cases put, to become the prey of the victor to the satisfaction and delight of the vanquished, and no reason or circumstance that you may plead will avail to shield or shelter you; for the victor dislikes doubtful friends, and such as will not help him at a pinch; and the vanquished will have nothing to say to you, since you would not share his fortunes sword in hand.

When Antiochus, at the instance of the Aetolians, passed into Greece in order to drive out the Romans, he sent envoys to the Achaians, who were friendly to the Romans, exhorting them to stand neutral. The Romans, on the other hand, urged them to take up arms on their behalf. The matter coming to be discussed in the Council of the Achaians, the legate of Antiochus again urged neutrality, whereupon the Roman envoy answered — 'Nothing can be less to your advantage than the course which has been recommended as the best and most useful for your State, namely, to refrain from taking any part in our war, for by standing aloof you will gain neither favor nor fame, but remain the prize of the victor.' And it will always happen that he who is not your friend will invite you to neutrality, while he who is your friend will call on you to declare yourself openly in arms. Irresolute Princes, to escape immediate danger, commonly follow the neutral path, in most instances to their destruction. But when you pronounce valiantly in favor of one side or other, if he to whom you give your adherence conquers, although he be powerful and you are at his mercy, still he is under obligations to you, and has become your friend; and none are so lost to shame as to destroy with manifest ingratitude, one who has helped them. Besides which, victories are never so complete that the victor can afford to disregard all considerations whatsoever, more especially considerations of justice. On the other hand, if he with whom you take part should lose, you will always be favorably regarded by him; while he can he will aid you, and you become his companion in a cause which may recover.

In the second case, namely, when both combatants are of such limited strength that whichever wins you have no cause to fear, it is all the more prudent for you to take a side, for you will then be ruining the one with the help of the other, who were he wise would endeavor to save him. If he whom you help conquers, he remains in your power, and with your aid he cannot but conquer.

And here let it be noted that a Prince should be careful never to join with one stronger than himself in attacking others, unless, as already said, he be driven to it by necessity. For if he whom you join prevails, you are at his mercy; and Princes, so far as in them lies, should avoid placing themselves at the mercy of others. The Venetians, although they might have declined the alliance, joined with France against the Duke of Milan, which brought about their ruin. But when an alliance cannot be avoided, as was the case with the Florentines when the Pope and Spain together led their armies to attack Lombardy, a Prince, for the reasons given, must take a side. Nor let it be supposed that any State can choose for itself a perfectly safe line of policy. On the contrary, it must reckon on every course which it may take being doubtful; for it happens in all human affairs that we never seek to escape one mischief without falling into another. Prudence therefore consists in knowing how to distinguish degrees of disadvantage, and in accepting a less evil as a good.

Again, a Prince should show himself a patron of merit, and should honor those who excel in every art. He ought accordingly to encourage his subjects by enabling them to pursue their callings, whether mercantile, agricultural, or any other, in security, so that this man shall not be deterred from beautifying his possessions from *the apprehension that they may be taken from him, or that other refrain from opening a trade through fear of taxes; and he should provide rewards for those who desire so to employ themselves, and for all who are disposed in any way to add to the greatness of his City or State.*

He ought, moreover, at suitable seasons of the year to entertain the people with festivals and shows. And because all cities are divided into guilds and companies, he should show attention to these societies, and sometimes take part in their meetings; offering an example of courtesy and munificence, but always maintaining the dignity of his station, which must under no circumstances be compromised.

Machiavelli offers some of his most dangerous advice here, urging neighbors to join in wars as a matter of course. The rationale that it is necessary as a defense is simply not consistent with the history of Switzerland, Costa Rica, or the more isolationist periods in the United States. Refraining from taking sides actually reduces the likelihood of invasion by neighbors. Trump wisely put NATO on notice that they should not expect the blank check approach that Clinton would continue. Clinton, even worse, repeatedly rattled her saber all over the campaign trail, threatening a dangerous no-fly zone project in Syria, despite warnings that such an operation could quickly start a shooting war with Russia and ultimately lead to nuclear annihilation. Johnson was even more isolationist than Trump and Stein campaigned as the sanest and most pacifist of all four.